RESISTANCES
OF PSYCHOANALYSIS

M E R I D I A N

Crossing Aesthetics

Werner Hamacher

& David E. Wellbery

Editors

Translated by
Peggy Kamuf,
Pascale-Anne Brault,
& Michael Naas

Stanford
University
Press

———

Stanford
California
1998

RESISTANCES
OF PSYCHOANALYSIS

Jacques Derrida

Assistance for the translation was provided
by the French Ministry of Culture

Originally published in France in 1996
as *Résistances de la psychanalyse*
by Editions Galilée
© 1996 by Editions Galilée

Printed in the United States of America

CIP data appear at the end of the book

Preface

Three essays on psychoanalysis, yes, to be sure, but first of all three essays on the logic of a singular coupling. Two kinds of resistance are in fact joined—that, at least, is the hypothesis: perhaps they give each other support these days; they ally with or relay each other, they draw up an obscure contract with each other.

On the one hand, there is the return, once again, of a resistance *to* psychoanalysis. There are countless signs that this resistance is growing and often novel in its social and institutional forms. It is as if, once assimilated or domesticated, psychoanalysis could be forgotten. It would then become something like an expired medication in the back room of a pharmacy: it can always be used in case of emergency or when supplies run out, but there are now better things on the market! Anyone today can see a resistance unfolding that is sometimes subtle and refined, an inventive or arrogant disavowal, often direct and massive, on the scale of the whole of European culture, which is the only one, finally, that has ever left its mark on psychoanalysis and which seems still today to be rejecting, fearing, or misunderstanding it now that its fashionable period (in fact, rather brief) is over. One could no doubt study the return of this resistance-*to*-psychoanalysis by taking one's inspiration from the Freudian discourse on "resistance-to-analysis." That path, however, will not be given priority in these three essays.

For there was perhaps, on the other hand, another resistance installed right away at the origin, like an auto-immune process, at the heart of psychoanalysis and already within the Freudian concept of "resistance-to-analysis": a resistance *of* psychoanalysis as we know it, a resistance to itself, in sum, which is just as inventive as the other. By coming to the aid of psychoanalysis despite itself, it constitutes perhaps one of the cards dealt to our time.

Prolegomena to the analysis of such a dealt card, these three essays were first of all "lectures," outlines of "readings" of Freud, Lacan, and Foucault.

Contents

RESISTANCES
OF PSYCHOANALYSIS

§ 1 Resistances

Must one resist?

And, first of all, psychoanalysis?

If it were necessary to resist analysis, one would still have to know whence comes this "one must" and what it means. One would still have to analyze it.

Is there "resistance to analysis," as the psychoanalysts say? Resistance to analysis is a theme about which psychoanalysts themselves seem to be making less noise these days. One may wonder why. It is as if, having been accused, more or less justly, of overusing it and thereby overcoming too quickly all questions or objections, which after *fast-analysis* are regularly filed away under symptoms of resistance, they were submitting to or preparing for other terms for the discussion.

Let us set aside this point, which is not merely a sociological one. By reactivating this question of resistance to analysis, let us try to go against the current and perhaps resist somewhat.

Must one—and if so, how?—analyze this resistance to analysis, if there is any, and the "there is" of this resistance? We would have to analyze a "one must," a "there is," and, above all, we would have to know whether what resists analysis does not also resist the analytic concept of "resistance to analysis." Can all "resistance to analysis" always be *reduced* to the interpretable status that analytic theory grants it or analyzes? Is there another resistance? Must there be another concept of resistance—and of analysis? And of resistance to analysis?

This is a lot of "one must's" and "there is's" and "resistances," which nevertheless seem to be organized around a provisionally stabilizing sense of *analysis*, namely, the sense laid down, in French rather than in another language, by psychoanalysis. Unless I am mistaken, only in French does one so commonly say "analysis" for "psychoanalysis." The history of this idiomatic formation would in itself deserve to be investigated.

Instead, it is an idiomatic interest, I could almost say an idiosyncratic interest, in the word "resistance" that I would like to share with you. At stake, in sum, is that which in me could learn to say "me" only by cultivating an idiom where—for reasons I do not understand very well but which I would like to try to elucidate a little with you this evening, as if I were *inanalysis* with you—the word "resistance" does not play just any role. Ever since I can remember, I have always loved this word. Why? How can one cultivate the word "resistance"? And want to save it at any price? Against analysis, to be sure, but *without* "analysis" and *from* analysis? And from translation? For I love the Franco-Latin word *résistance* inasmuch as it resists translation and even, for me, its translation into or its transparency in French, in my "own" language.

This word, which resonated in my desire and my imagination as the most beautiful word in the politics and history of this country, this word loaded with all the pathos of my nostalgia, as if, at any cost, I would like not to have missed blowing up trains, tanks, and headquarters between 1940 and 1945—why and how did it come to attract, like a magnet, so many other meanings, virtues, semantic or disseminal chances? I am going to tell you which ones even if I cannot discern the secret of my inconsolable nostalgia—which thus remains to be analyzed or which resists analysis, a little like the navel of a dream.

Why have I always dreamed of resistance? And why should one worry here about a navel?

Everything seems to be pointing—but don't worry too much—toward a lecture on the word *résistance*, a self-satisfied and navel-gazing look at a thoroughly French word, at its roots in the history of this country and, worse, at my professed love for the word and perhaps for the thing—or at *my* resistance to analysis. I do not promise not to give in at all to the temptation, but I will try, as I proceed, to suggest some other things: as nonidiomatic as possible, they will respond, I hope, both to the title and thus to the contract of this colloquium, to the general concept of analysis, and, above all, to the fine lecture by Miguel Giusti.

I more or less repeat, then, my question: Why dream of resistance? And should one still be concerned with the navel of a dream?

1. The Taste of a Solution

Miguel Giusti (see headnote, p. 119) began by quoting Goethe, from whom he drew his first guiding threads regarding what is untangled by analysis, by *analysis* as untangling, untying, detaching, freeing, even liberation—and thus also, let us not forget, as *solution*. The Greek word *analuein*, as is well known, means to untie and thus to dissolve the link. It can thus be rigorously approached, if not translated, by the Latin *solvere* (to detach, deliver, absolve, or acquit). Both *solutio* and *resolutio* have the sense of dissolution, dissolved tie, extrication, disengagement, or acquittal (for example, from debt) *and* that of solution of a problem: explanation or unveiling. The *solutio linguae* is also the tongue untied.

Since Miguel Giusti has named Goethe's *geistige Band*, permit me to evoke in my turn a great reader of Goethe, someone who cited him often, as did Heidegger, with whom he shares at least this priceless debt and, by the same token, other less apparent commitments. When he speaks of the navel of the dream, with regard to the "Dream of Irma's Injection," Freud confesses a feeling, a premonition (*Ich ahne*, he writes).[1] The confession has its natural place in a note added after a certain delay. Freud's tone and the status of this note are indeed those of a confession. Remorse or repentance, the note is offered after the fact but, such as it is, to analysis. It calls upon the reader as witness in the way one might address oneself to a confessor or to some transferential addressee, some would say to an analyst, assuming that a reader is not always an analyst. Freud, then, has the premonition (*Ich ahne*) that something exceeds the analysis. The interpretation, the analytic deciphering, the *Deutung* of a certain fragment did not go far enough: a hidden meaning (*verborgene Sinn*) exceeds the analysis. Let us say for the moment that the meaning *exceeds* and not that it *resists* analysis: the concept of resistance to analysis has in fact another import and belongs to another code in the Freudian discourse, even though—and we will get to this—it appears in the same context and is not without relation to this excess.

In this note, moreover, Freud seems to have no doubts that this hidden thing has a sense. For the moment, this sense appears to be secret or dissimulated (*verborgene Sinn*), but what still remains out of range cannot not be transfixed with sense. The inaccessible secret is some sense, it is full of sense. In other words, for the moment the secret refuses analysis, but as sense it is analyzable; *it is homogeneous to the order of the analyzable. It comes under psychoanalytic reason. Psychoanalytic reason as hermeneutic reason.* I underscore this trait and, in proposing to problematize it, I hope to go in the same direction as Miguel Giusti, although the path I am following is, as too often, indirect. I would like to try to join up with him in the vicinity where, near his conclusion, he evoked "discordant contemporary voices" who engage and argue with each other in, I quote him, "the discussion of the very sense of rationality, that is, the controversy around sense, the limits, or the illusions of reason," a discussion that could be interpreted, he continues, "as a *topical discussion* whereby . . . the exercise of dialogue with the tradition, which Aristotle called the art of dialectic, is prolonged."

For a very provisional starting point, let us identify in a singular passage from *The Interpretation of Dreams* certain questions that open from a distance onto what could be called the Freudian analytic, topic, and dialectic. I will not interrogate directly (as is done too little in France, though more often in the Anglo-Saxon analytic milieu) Freud's implicit epistemology, his models of analysis, argumentation, demonstration, his logic of proof, his rhetoric, narratic, and, if you will, his analytic and dialectic. Without doing so directly, but once again at an angle, I hope to specify what may be the principle of this task. On the horizon will stand the question of whether psychoanalysis—whether the idea of analysis that gives it its name—finds suitable lodging in the history of reason, in what is at issue there between analytic and dialectic.

This analytic concern (to render reason of sense as sense, even if it is hidden—*verborgene Sinn,* says the note in question) merges here with a *hermeneutic* drive or watchword. In truth, with the principle of reason itself, there where it prescribes that one must "render reason," *reddere rationem,* at any cost. One must *render.* Fidelity to sense, duty, debt, sense of required restitution, of the restitution of the sense of sense: all this seems all the more remarkable in that Freud is soon going to radicalize this notation. He is going to proceed to a generalization by taking one more step. And this is what he will call the navel of the dream.

This step will be in truth a leap.

I will not say anything new about this "Dream of Irma's Injection." The sense of this text, if not of this dream—I repeat, the sense of this text, if it has any—will have surely been exhausted for some time now by the enormous analytic literature that, throughout the world, has submitted it to investment and investigation from every angle. My only alibi with which to plead the innocence or the freshness of my modest reading is that this reading is concerned, precisely, with something other, perhaps, than sense itself—and thus with something other than analysis, a certain analysis, something that, in another sense, perhaps, resists analysis, a certain analysis. I will not claim to teach anything to anyone, but rather will re-pose the question of sense and of analysis, of a certain determination of sense and of analysis, and will do it with the example, the exemplary example as regards analysis, of a certain solution (*Lösung*).

Freud, then, has just remarked that the analysis of this fragment had not been "carried" (*geführt*) far enough: there would thus still be some reserve of sense and movement for going further. Freud then makes two fascinating remarks—one could even call them passionate—whose juxtaposition and heterogeneity would deserve interminable analysis. The two remarks are separated in the original text by a period and a dash (all of which disappear in the French translation, at least in the first translation, which therefore must be set aside if one is interested in this passage).

First Remark: Freud's Wife/Woman Between Three and Four

We must pause a moment at what Freud suggests about a *square of women*. In the register of the reserve of sense and of the provisionally interrupted analysis, Freud notes curiously that, had he pursued the comparison (*Vergleichung*) between the three women, he would surely have been led far afield. Why? He does not say, not really. Why would he risk losing his way? Why is he even sure of this? Why is he so afraid of what he seems so sure? Why would he go astray by comparing the three women? And, above all, what does he know? How can he know that he would go astray where he confesses or claims to confess that he didn't go see, not far enough?

Right here, at this point, it would not be impossible to speak of resistance to analysis. Moreover, in the paragraph of the main text Freud comments upon, at the signal for the note, Freud has said a little more, just barely, about his own resistance, but in noting that what these three women had in common was already, precisely, a certain resistance to analysis. We will read this paragraph. As we all know, Freud is in the process of analyzing his own dream, a dream that he himself will end up by presenting, in conclusion, as a defense in the form of kettle logic, to wit: (1) the kettle I'm returning to you is intact; (2) what is more, the holes were already in it when I borrowed it, and (3) besides, you never lent me a kettle. I recall as well that it is a matter of posing as a *general thesis* that, after a complete analysis (*nach vollendeter Deutungsarbeit*), every dream can be recognized as the fulfillment of a wish. Although Freud still maintains this here, things will get more complicated later on, notably in *Beyond the Pleasure Principle*, which will also complicate, as we shall see, the question of sense. Thus of analysis. The complete analysis, says Freud for the moment, reveals the secret sense of the dream as the fulfillment of a wish. But Freud has also just specified with great insistence that he is not at all claiming to have totally unveiled (*vollständig entdeckt*) the sense of this dream (*den Sinn dieses Traums*). He is not claiming, far from it, that his analytical interpretation is "without a gap" (*lückenlose*) (120– 21). Indeed, a note several pages earlier said that he of course does not think it a good idea to report everything that occurred to him during the work of interpretation. No less fundamentally, before we quote the paragraph on the three or four women and their common resistance to analysis, we must recall that everything here is *concentrated* and at the same time *dissolved* in a solution (*Lösung*), a chemical solution but also—and Freud takes this sense into account in the interpretation of his dream—the solution of a problem (it's the same word, *Lösung*), an analytic solution. An analytic solution untangles, resolves, even absolves; it undoes the symptomatic or etiological knot. The same word (solution, analytic resolution, *Lösung*) is valid for the drug and for the end of the analysis. And the reason Freud reproaches Irma in the course of the dream, the reason he reproaches Irma's resistance, is that she has not accepted *his solution*. He says so himself: "[I] reproach her for not having accepted my 'solution' yet. I said to her: 'If you still get pains, it's really only your fault (*deine eigene Schuld*)' " (107). He says this to her in the dream. It is in the dream that he formulates this reproach and thereby refuses to acquit the other of her debt, to absolve her of her fault (*Schuld*), namely, her fault at not having accepted the proposed solution. For that is the *fault* for which the patient is culpable, accountable, responsible, which is to say, by this failing, properly bound.

In passing, after having quoted this part of the dream, he re- marks (this is another confession of the wakeful Freud): "I might have said this to her in waking life, and I may actually have done so. It was my view at that time (though I have since recognized it as a wrong one) that my task was fulfilled when I had informed a patient of the hidden meaning of his symptoms [once again, *den verborgenen Sinn ihrer Symptome*]: I considered that I was not responsible [*nicht mehr verantwortlich*] for whether he accepted the solution [*Lösung*] or not—though this was what success depended on" (108).

In other words, I am responsible for the analytic solution (*Lösung*) but not for the resistance of the patient, who can refuse it and who is thus alone responsible, culpable, accountable for his resistance. Here again, Freud confesses an error. He has fortunately overcome it since, he says; it had merely made his life easier. Here now is the paragraph that turns around the three women *to be compared*, the departure of the graces or disgraces to which a fourth, indispensable dimension must be added, the term of a fourth character: Freud's own wife. Not only because the dream anticipates, as Freud notes, his wife's birthday, when the couple received a crowd of guests in the large hall at Bellevue—including Irma. But also because, in yet another note, Freud adds to a governess whom he had once had as a patient and to Irma's good friend, whom he has just mentioned, a third person (who is thus a fourth if one counts Irma—and I would say, in a dogmatic and elliptical fashion for the moment, that what I would like to talk about this evening, under the title of resistances, of resistance to analysis, of a certain resistance to a certain analysis, is a passage, through the untangling of a knot, *between the three and the four*). This third-fourth person is his wife, whose birthday is coming up:

> The still unexplained complaint about *pains in the abdomen* could also be traced back to this third figure. The person in question was, of course [*natürlich*, missing in the French translation], my own wife; the pains in the abdomen reminded me of one of the occasions on which I had noticed her bashfulness. I was forced to admit [*mir eingestehen*: yet another confession] that I was not treating either Irma or my wife very kindly in this dream; but it should be observed by way of excuse [*zu meiner Entschuldigung*] that I was measuring them both by the standard of the good and amenable patient [*am Ideal der braven, gefügigen Patientin*]. (110)

This note precedes the note on the *omphalos* of the dream. Here, then, is the announced paragraph:

> I had been comparing my patient Irma with two other people [one of whom, then, silently reminds him of his wife] who would also have

been recalcitrant to treatment [*sträuben*, to stand on end, to resist; Freud often uses this verb, as he does in the recital of the dream that begins our paragraph, where he describes Irma's reluctance to open her mouth, a "recalcitrance" like that of women who wear dentures, when he reproaches her for not having accepted his *Lösung*]. What could the reason have been for my having exchanged her in the dream for her friend? [*Was kann es für Sinn haben?*, that is: "What does this mean?"; "What sense can it have?"] Perhaps it was that I should have *liked* to exchange her: either I felt more sympathetic towards her friend or had a higher opinion of her intelligence. For Irma seemed to me foolish because she had not accepted my solution [*meine Lösung nicht akzeptiert*]. Her friend would have been wiser, that is to say she would have yielded sooner [by implication, to my advice, to my demand—or to my advances]. She would then have *opened her mouth properly*, and have told me [*erzählen*] more than Irma. (110–11)

Freud thus gives the example of a law. Which law? The one that in general commands one to interpret as resistance to analysis, to the solution, to the resolution (*Lösung*), the reservation of anyone who does not accept *your* solution.

(Such a law, let it be said in parentheses, reinscribes all analysis in a relation of forces and all interpretation in the *politics* of a *polemos* and an *eros*, in the seduction—let us risk this word—of an irreducible *poleros*. To analyze anything whatsoever, anyone whatsoever, for anyone whatsoever, would mean saying to the other: choose my solution, prefer my solution, take my solution, love my solution; you will be in the truth if you do not resist my solution. Placing what I say *en abyme*, it seems to me, I will add that one can dispute the ineluctable truth of this scene, possibly *in the name of the truth*, only in disavowal; one can oppose to it only disavowal, but a disavowal in the name of the truth is not just any disavowal, whence the abyss—that's the whole problem. Oh, the scholar, the philosopher, and above all the analyst will doubtless disagree with what I have just said, and will do so by claiming that the objective truth, or the truth of being or analytic neutrality, removes the passions of resistance, disavowal, and appropriation from this *poleros* and this duel. To avoid too much precipitation, I would say in a word that the only limit to this *poleros*, to this condensation of the *political*, *polemos*, and *eros*, and the only suspension of this analytic seduction is another concept of resistance or rather of *remaining* [*restance*], a *restanalysis* toward which I am orienting this lecture— and whose premises or implications will, I hope, become clear little by little. I close this anticipatory parenthesis.)

This law of the *poleros* is given an example here. Freud tells us why he would have preferred the other, the other woman: because she would have spoken to him better, in other words, she would have *spoken* to him more [*elle lui aurait* dit *davantage*], which in ordinary French means that she pleased him more. She was more to his taste, she who would have been docile enough to accept his solution and thus not to resist him. As Freud makes sufficiently clear, all of these things, beginning with the solution, pass by way of the mouth, with or without dentures.

At no moment does Freud have even an inkling that a resistance might be, in this context, something other than a resistance to his solution, to his analysis, or, beyond this context and in general, that a resistance might be something other than a resistance full of meaning to an analysis full of meaning. Even if it is definitive, resistance belongs, along with what it resists, to the order of sense, of a sense whose secret is only the hidden secret, the dissimulated meaning, the veiled truth: to be interpreted, analyzed, made explicit, explained.

Second Remark: The Omphalos

Right after the comparison between these two, three, or four women, right after the passage from the triangle to the square, we come then (if we can still say that) to this inaccessible *topos*. Giving rhythm to his discourse with an interesting punctuation (a period followed by a dash indicates that one is changing registers and levels), Freud advances the famous proposition about the umbilicus, the *Nabel* of the dream. Such a proposition, this time, no longer concerns a provisional limit, a reserve of meaning that still awaits us; it concerns rather a night, an absolute unknown that is originarily, congenitally bound or tied (but also in itself unbound because ab-solute) to the essence and to the birth of the dream, attached to the place from which it departs and of which it keeps the birthmark: the umbilicus, the omphalic place is the place of a *tie*, a knot-scar that keeps the memory of a cut and even of a severed thread at birth. And the *general* proposition, the assertion in the form of an unconditionally posed law, which is itself cut off from its context and detached from the fragment of the dream that gives it its pretext, is the assertion according to which *every* dream, *always*, carries within it at least one place (*eine Stelle*), one marked *topos* that situates it as *unergründlich, gleichsam einen Nabel*: impenetrable, unfathomable, unanalyzable, like a navel, an *omphalos*. And Freud adds, so as better to suture or sew the thing up, that through this place it is knotted, attached, connected, or suspended (*zusammenhängt*, which implies once again the figure of the knot, of the knotted thread) with the unknown (*mit dem Unerkannten*: the French translation reads here "the unknowable" instead of the unknown, the nonrecognized, but it does give one the sense of the insoluble, unsolvable, indissoluble character, because ab-solute, of this unknottable knot).

Because it is a matter here of analysis, of tying and untying, let us insist, for the moment at least, more on the knotting and less on the hole that it sutures. Lacan is more interested in the gap and the carved-out localization of the umbilical hole. At the beginning of *The Four Fundamental Concepts of Psychoanalysis*, he writes: "What Freud calls the navel—*the navel of the dreams*, he writes, to designate their ultimately unknown centre—which is simply, like the same anatomical navel that represents it, that gap of which I have already spoken."[2]

What forever exceeds the analysis of the dream is indeed a knot that cannot be untied, a thread that, even if it is cut, like an umbilical cord, nevertheless remains forever knotted, right on the body, at the place of the navel. The scar is a knot against which analysis can do nothing. I believe this very well-known passage deserves to be reread in this context *for two reasons*.

In the *first place*, not so as to translate *Deutung* too quickly by analysis, but because the Penelopian or counter-Penelopian task of the *Deutung*, which is, after all, an analysis (Freud recalled this several pages earlier when he wrote that the interpretation he is inaugurating is indeed an analysis at least insofar as it deals with details—he writes, in French, that "it employs interpretation *en détail* and not *en masse*" [104]), is a knot, threads to be untied, and *untied where there has been a cut*. (It is thus always a matter for us of thinking how the cut can tie a knot or, inversely, how the link can be interruption itself. And of thinking "resistance" starting from the necessity of what does anything but *play* with the paradox or the aporia.)

In the *second place*, because we ought to link this passage to a connected passage from the *Traumdeutung* that, it seems, allows one to draw closer to what forms literally the weave or shuttle of this text. This is found in the subchapter "Forgetting of Dreams," at the beginning of chapter 7, "The Psychology of the Dream-Processes." Freud has just pointed out that most dreams, although not all, do not require over-interpretation or over-analysis (*Uberdeutung*) and that all dreams do not lend themselves to an *anagogic* interpretation (*anagogische Deutung*), that is, to an interpretation that, like analysis, goes back (*ana*) to the highest, the most originary, the most archaic, or the most profound. Freud here uses a word, "anagogic," that is not his own. The word comes from someone he is in the process of refuting and who answers to the very beautiful name of Silberer. Silberer distinguished between two types of interpretation. "Psychoanalytic" interpretation (the word is Silberer's) gives to the dream, says Freud explaining Silberer, a meaning (*Sinn*), most often a meaning that refers to infantile sexuality. As for "anagogic" interpretation, it concerns the depth of meaning, the profound seriousness of the thoughts that fill out the dream, the fullness of meaning that the dream takes as its fabric, its text, or its material (*Stoff*). To dismiss this distinction and this terminology, Freud replies: all dreams do not require over-interpretation (*Uberdeutung*); they do not all lend themselves to this anagogy invoked by a Silberer who is accused, moreover, not only of lacking empirical proof but also of giving in to allegorical readings. Freud goes further: to the question of whether every dream can be submitted to *Deutung*, to interpretive analysis, he says that he answers "no." And it is in order to justify this "no" that he invokes resistances.

He then gives to these resistances the name that will continue to be theirs in a number of texts: *Widerstände*. If certain dreams, however, refuse to submit to interpretation, it is not at all because they lack meaning; it's because the work of interpretive analysis (*Deutungsarbeit*) has ranged against it (*gegen sich*) psychical powers (*psychische Mächte*) that are responsible for the displacements and disguises of the dream. Freud identifies very well the question we were talking about a moment ago. It is, he says, the question of a relation of forces (*eine Frage des Kräfteverhältnisses*). That *against* which intellectual curiosity (which is also a force), discipline, psychological knowledge, analytic experience have to struggle is indeed "internal resistances" (*innere Widerstände*). It is thus a matter of mastering these resistances by opposing them, by buttressing oneself with an antithesis.

However, like the resistance that we meet with in analysis, this relation of forces *has meaning. And truth.* By overcoming resistances, we accede to oneiric formations full of meaning (*sinnreiche*). Progress is an approach to, an approximation of this meaning (*Ahnung dieses Sinnes*). Resistance must be interpreted; it has as much meaning as what it opposes; it is just as charged with meaning and thus just as interpretable as that which it disguises or displaces: in truth, it has *the same meaning*, but dialectically or polemically adverse, if one can say that.

At this point in Freud's rhetoric, as well as in his argumentative logic, the same rupture is produced, at least in appearance, that we saw in the previous note, hundreds of pages earlier. After having evoked the progressive approximation (*Ahnung*) of a meaning that was only provisionally held at a distance, barred, or disguised by resistances and that nevertheless continues always to promise itself to analysis, across the resistances themselves, Freud seems to pose an absolute limit to this progress (which one can, moreover, trans-

late and enlarge into the progress of reason in general)—and he
names the *omphalos* once again. It is difficult to decide whether the
"one must" (*man muss*), which confers modality on the utterance,
records an unsurpassable limit as a *Factum* or a *Fatum*, or whether
it it a "one must" of duty that institutes what one *must* do, which is
not to go beyond or, if you prefer, what one *must not* do, which is to
go beyond, because that has no meaning.[3]

The difference between the two modalities points to the enormous stakes. In the first case, the *Factum* or the *Fatum prevents us
without prohibiting us* from going beyond; since it concerns an
external prevention of some sort, one may assume that there is
meaning beyond, that there is a sense in going beyond, even if one
cannot do it. In the second case, a structural limit prohibits us from
going beyond and thus leaves the presumption of sense undecided.
But first we should translate this passage:

> There is often a passage [a place, *eine Stelle*] in even the most thor-
> oughly interpreted dream which has to be [*man muss*] left obscure
> [*muss man oft eine Stelle im Dunkel lassen*]; this is because we become
> aware during the work of interpretation that at that point there is a
> tangle [*Knäuel*, like a ball of yarn] of dream-thoughts which cannot be
> unravelled [*der sich nicht entwirren will*] and which moreover adds
> nothing to our knowledge of the content of the dream. This is the
> dream's navel [*der Nabel des Traums*], the spot where it reaches down
> into the unknown. The dream-thoughts to which we are led by
> interpretation cannot, from the nature of things, have any definite
> endings [*mussen bleiben ohne Abschluss*]; they are bound to branch out
> in every direction into the intricate network [*in die netzartige Ver-
> strickung*] of our world of thought. It is at some point where this
> meshwork [*Geflecht*] is particularly close that the dream-wish grows
> up, like a mushroom out of its mycelium. (525)

In the knowing meshwork of its own fabric, this text remains just
as enigmatic as what it is talking about, the *omphalos*. It places it *en
abyme*. We will retain what concerns our motif: analysis.

   1. First, there is a tireless insistence on the texture of interwoven
threads, on a skein of knots that cannot be untangled: it is *Geflecht,*

translated here as "meshwork," the word whose woof or warp Heidegger followed into decisive places for thought; it is also *die netzartige Verstrickung*, the *Knäuel*, *Nabel*, and so forth. The density of this rhetoric of thread and knot interests us because it appeals to and challenges analysis as a methodical operation of unknotting and technique of untying. It is all a matter of knowing how to pull threads, pull on the threads, according to the art of the weaver, which Plato's *Statesman* made into a royal paradigm: for the analytic division (*diairesis*), for dialectic, for the royal science (*e basilikē technē*) of the statesman (311C). I refer you to a passage in the very fine book by Samuel Weber, *The Legend of Freud*,[4] which rigorously studies from another point of view the meshwork of these figures of umbilical meshwork, not overlooking that "Weber" also means "weaver" (following an etymology it perhaps has in common with the Greek *uphē, uphen*, or *uphainō*, for woven cloth and "to weave"), nor that Mephistopheles, taken for Faust (according to Goethe, as Miguel Giusti reminded us at the outset), compared the "fabrication of thought" to a *Weber-Meisterstück*, to a weaver's masterpiece that handles thousands of threads (*Fäden*), plies the shuttle (*Schifflein*), forming thousands of links and knots (*Verbindungen*) at a single stroke (*Schlag*).

2. Another remark is that this birthplace is assigned to the wish or desire of the dream. Freud tells us that the dream-wish arises, grows up, surges forth (*erhebt sich*) at the densest point of this *Geflecht*, of this meshwork, like a mushroom out of its mycelium. The place of origin of this desire would thus be the very place where the analysis must come to a halt, the place that must be left in obscurity (*muss man im Dunkel lassen*). And this place would be a knot or a tangled mass of threads, in short, an unanalyzable synthesis.

3. A last remark in the form of a divided question in effect concerns this *topic*. Such a question, which I will deliberately leave suspended, is in fact divided:

A. Is this limit of analysis, instead of being the origin of the dream-wish, a resistance to analysis? (It would then be provi-

sional and captured in an archivable history: for example, Freud
has just related how, years later, he was able to interpret more
easily some of his recorded dreams because in the meantime he
had overcome resistances [*Widerstände*] in his interior life.) Or is
this limit of analysis instead attached, in some irreducible and
ahistorical way, to the structure of the dream-wish, which must
be born, like a mushroom, at the point of greatest density of a
meshwork destined to obscurity? If one transposes these first two
hypotheses into a history of reason, the distinction between
them is like that between, on the one side, an Enlightenment
progressivism, which hopes for an analysis that will continue to
gain ground on initial obscurity to the degree that it removes
resistances and liberates, unbinds, emancipates, as does every
analysis, and, on the other side, a sort of fatalism or pessimism of
desire that reckons with a portion of darkness and situates the
unanalyzable as its very resource.

B. But in the two hypotheses, the first question can be divided again or, if you like, it can be analyzed: in both cases one
may wonder whether the in-soluble knot, the umbilicus, is of the
stuff of sense or whether it remains radically heterogeneous, in
its very secret, to signifiable sense, as well as to the signifier, and
one may also wonder whether what discourages the analyst, provisionally or definitively, is homogeneous or not with the space
of analytic work, the work of interpretation (*Deutungsarbeit*).

We will have neither the time nor the means to take up here this
ordered series of hypotheses, particularly within Freud's text. One
would have to read closely, among other things, all Freud's earlier
and later texts on resistance. One would have to take account of the
fact that psychoanalysis began by analyzing a resistance to hypnotic
suggestion. When he judged the counter-suggestion with which
the patient defended herself or himself against hypnosis to be the
exercise of a right and found this legitimate resistance to be insurmountable, Freud invented, so to speak, psychoanalysis, a technique that is in principle nonhypnotic. This does not mean that it
was nonviolent (recall what we were saying about the relation of

forces), but that it was concerned in principle with a new ethic of analysis. Beginning with *Studies on Hysteria*, Freud proposes a whole catalog of resistances to analysis, that is, of defenses to be conquered when a representation is repressed out of consciousness and out of memory: "The psychical trace of it was apparently lost to view." But, says Freud, "that trace must be there." "If I endeavored to direct the patient's attention to it [this trace], I became aware, in the form of *resistance*, of the same force as had shown itself in the form of *repulsion* when the symptom was generated."⁵ It is thus a trace that resists analysis. And even as he explains the success of what he called the "pressure technique" (281) against the "resistance to association" (270) (pressure of the hand on the forehead along with the injunction to speak, to declare the images and ideas that come to mind, the pressing prohibition against remaining silent), Freud proposes a sort of catalog of "the different forms in which this resistance appears" (278). When the resistance is prolonged, when one has not succeeded in transforming the patient, the resister, into a "collaborator" (that is Freud's word) to whom one supplies explanations and in whom one arouses an investigator's objective interest in himself (thus already by substituting one motif for another), when one has not managed to "push back his resistance, resting . . . on an affective basis," then "the most powerful lever," "after we have discovered the motives for his defense [therefore for this 'resistance'], is to deprive them of their value or even to replace them by more powerful ones" (282).

It is thus not a matter of simply and in total neutrality substituting an unveiled truth for what resists it, but rather of leading the patient to awareness [*la prise de conscience*] by actively and energetically using counter-resistances, other antagonistic forces, through an effective intervention in a field of forces. Freud always maintained that resistance could not be removed by the simple discovery of the truth or by the simple revelation to the patient of the true meaning of a symptom. At this point, analysis of a resistance does not consist in a theoretical explanation of the origin and the elements of a defense symptom, but in an unbinding dissolution, an effective and affective practical analysis of the resistance broken down in its force and displaced in its locus—resistance not only comprehended and communicated in its *intelligibility*, but transformed, transposed, transfigured.

At stake, then, are sense and truth.

Once this phase is attained, Freud tells us, there are no more general rules; this analytic technique can no longer be formalized as a technique of counter-resistances. I will cite a sentence that could cover the whole field in which analysis is interested *as psychoanalysis*, that is, all the disciplines and all the discursive situations where the question of analysis is in play: teaching, for example, the teaching of philosophy—with the problems of analytic and dialectic that Miguel Giusti described so well, and with its ideal of Reason and of Enlightenment (I will return later to the question of Enlightenment)—but also religion, with the concern for truth or avowal that institutes, for example, confession:

> This no doubt is where it ceases to be possible to state psychotherapeutic activity in formulas. One works to the best of one's power, as an elucidator (where ignorance has given rise to fear), as a teacher, as the representative of a freer or superior view of the world, as a father confessor who gives absolution, as it were, by a continuance of his sympathy and respect after the confession has been made. (282)

If, however, resistance is not lifted by the revelation of its meaning, then, beyond all these discursive and intellectual situations that belong to the order of consciousness, it can only be lifted by the intervention of an affective factor. Freud insists on this in the very next sentence:

> Besides the intellectual motives which we mobilize to overcome the resistance, there is an affective factor, the personal influence of the physician, which we can seldom do without, and in a number of cases the latter alone is in a position to remove the resistance. The situation here is no different from what it is elsewhere in medicine and there is no therapeutic procedure of which one may say that it can do entirely without the co-operation of this personal factor. (283)

In the context of our discussion, this affects the whole philosophical history of analysis, from the royal weaver of the Platonic dialectic to the dialectic of the Hegelian presupposition, from the topics and analytics of Aristotle to Kant's transcendental analytic and the reckoning with *a priori* synthetic judgment. This whole history of philosophy, as such, would belong to the order of representation or of ideational consciousness; it could not intervene, at least as such, in an effective and affective fashion, in a *decisive* fashion to remove resistance of any sort. The two analyses would remain heterogeneous. The problematic of philosophical analysis—or of everything of which it is the type and the model— could at most, and *to the extent that* this philosophical analysis is invested with desire and motivations, *work toward* [concourir à] the lifting of such resistances.

One would thus be tempted to think that the event of psychoanalysis was the advent, under the same name, of *another concept of analysis.* Of a concept different from the one that has held sway in the history of philosophy, logic, science. And at the same time a topical displacement would have occurred in all the concepts that form a system with it. Beginning with the concept of truth. Is there a tradition of analysis in general? If there was no unity of the concept of analysis, there would be no tradition—from philosophy to psychoanalysis. Not one tradition, not a single one.

But things are surely not so simple. For several reasons:

1. Under the old name, the paleonym "analysis," Freud did not introduce or invent a new concept, supposing that such a thing ever exists. Who, besides God, has ever *created*, literally "created," a concept? Freud had no choice, if he wished to make himself understood, but to inherit from tradition. He had no choice but to keep the *two motifs* that are constitutive for every concept of analysis.

The concurrence of these two motifs figures in the figure from the Greek language, namely, *analuein.* There is, *on the one hand,* what could be called the *archeological* or *anagogical* motif, which is marked in the movement of *ana* (recurrent return toward the principial, the most originary, the simplest, the elementary, or the detail that cannot be broken down); and, *on the other hand,* a motif that could be nicknamed *lytic, lytological,* or *philolytic,* marked in the *lysis* (breaking down, untying, unknotting, deliverance, solution, dissolution or absolution, and, by the same token, final completion). Thus the *archeological* motif of analysis is doubled by an *eschatological* movement, as if analysis were the bearer of extreme death and the last word, just as the archeological motif, in view of the originary, is turned toward birth.

2. Keeping as legacy the two motifs of this axiomatics—which is that of science no less than of philosophy—Freud was neither able nor willing to inaugurate a *new concept of analysis*. He had to justify his discourse and his institution before the tribunal of traditional analysis, before its norms and its law. To this extent, at least, his discourse remains answerable to all the logico-epistemological questions to which we alluded a moment ago.

3. If things are so *entangled*, if the *Geflecht* affects the whole of this historical situation, it is because this imbrication of the psychoanalytic concept in the traditional concept of analysis cannot be disentangled for more reasons than those we have just indicated. If one considers that psychoanalysis developed not only as the analysis of individual psychic resistances but as a practical analysis of the cultural, political, and social resistances represented by hegemonic discourses, notably in the form of its philosophical or scientific knowledge, it would have been necessary, if this history were to form *one* history and if it were to be unified in *one tradition*, for psychoanalysis itself to have a *unified* concept of resistance, of its logic and its topic.

And this was never the case. Such, in any case, is my hypothesis.

If it is true that the concept of *resistance to analysis* cannot unify itself, for nonaccidental or noncontingent reasons, then the concept of analysis and of psychoanalytic analysis, the very concept of *psychoanalysis* will have known the same fate. Being determined, if one can say that, only in adversity and in relation to what resists it, psychoanalysis will never gather itself into the unity of a concept or a task. If there is not *one* resistance, there is not "*la* psychanalyse"— whether one understands it here as system of theoretical norms or as a charter of institutional practices.[6]

If this is indeed the way it is, this situation does not necessarily translate a failure. There is also here a chance for success, with no need to dramatize things. I don't believe one needs to turn this disjunction, in this case or any other, into bad drama. The inability to gather oneself, to identify with oneself, to unify oneself, all of this is perhaps tragedy itself, but it is also (the) chance and if there is no reason to dramatize, it is not only because that serves no purpose but also because it has not the least pertinence for this alliance of destiny, namely tragedy, and chance as the possible or the aleatory.

To say that psychoanalysis does not have *the* concept of what it itself is in its auto-identification, because it cannot give itself a concept of resistance, is certainly not to describe a paralysis of psychoanalysis, at least not a banal and negative paralysis. (There is also another logic of *paralysis* that some time ago, in "Pas," I distinguished from the logic of analysis.)[7] It gives movement, it gives one to think and to move: with regard to auto-interpretation or, if one prefers, the auto-interpretation of psychoanalysis, but also with regard to *its* other, the adversary to which it opposed itself and the resistance of the traditional concept of analysis which it challenged.

This impossibility of unifying the concept of resistance and of identifying the place of its insistence has never been a secret, especially not for Freud. Besides all of the initial hesitations that we have just pointed out in the *Studies on Hysteria* and in *The Interpretation of Dreams*, we know that much later, in the Addenda to "Inhibition, Symptom, Anxiety" (1926), Freud recognizes no fewer than *five* types of resistance. They call for very different analytic strategies. These are distinguished topically and dynamically, and they have corollaries in five topico-dynamic regulations of analysis.

Three types of resistance proceed from the ego, the id, and the superego. Those that come from ego, in other words from the egological subject and from a *cogito* that is not necessarily conscious through and through, are also of three sorts and differ among themselves as regards the dynamic. One has to do with repression, and this is the case Freud deals with most extensively. Another has to do with transference and sometimes retriggers repression because it consolidates repression rather than recalling it. Finally, the third egological resistance, of a wholly other kind, integrates the symptom into the ego and seeks a benefit in the illness. (Let me say in an aside that I wonder who does not do that, what ego does not institute itself and does not last by means of this form of resistance, and on what confused concept of illness one is relying when one describes this ruse as an interesting singularity.)

We have here a virtual program for transcribing all the possibilities of resistance into the order of the philosophic and scientific self, and, in general, into the order of what could be called the *cogito* of *homo analyticus*, the man of analysis.

As for the resistance that comes from the *id*, it calls for the analytic work that Freud names *Durcharbeitung*. (*Perlaboration* is the standard French translation: the English "working through" would be clearer, more analytic, more "French.") In the course of this laborious traversal, the subject sometimes becomes entrenched in resistance. Repression still persists, it insists, it resists even when the resistance of the ego has already been lifted. At that moment, one sees that the intellectual, theoretical, philosophical, ideal, or ideational acceptance of the analytic interpretation does not suffice to lift repression, which is, according to Freud, the ultimate source of resistance. What remains still to be conquered is the repetition compulsion—to which we will return in a moment because it deserves, in my opinion, to be treated in a special way. Finally, Freud mentions a fifth resistance, that of the superego, which opposes guilt to cure: the need to be punished can become intransigent, confession or interpretation can slide around or on the surface of this resistance.

All these organized types of resistance can be distinguished by a logical, conceptual, methodical analysis, but in reality they are tangled up with and overdetermine each other. Above all—this is in my view the most decisive scansion and will thus fold my lecture in two—when one seeks to determine the unity of this concept, which serves as a semantic support or paradigmatic reference for the five forms of resistance, one encounters a "resistance to analysis" that figures *both* the most resistant resistance, resistance par excellence, hyperbolic resistance, *and* the one that disorganizes the very principle, the constitutive idea of psychoanalysis as analysis of resistances.

(There is nothing very surprising in this logic, for which we could find other examples: the principle of a series also transcends it and, withdrawn from the meaning that it confers, it comes to deprive of meaning the very thing to which it gives meaning.) One could say, in fact, that the multiplicity of resistances does not necessarily threaten the concept of resistance. The latter would be a genus with several species. Its unity of meaning and place, as well as its validity, would even be confirmed by this diffraction: it itself, the same, is what one would find again throughout.

But in order to determine this supporting sense, one must follow the guiding thread of the strongest resistance or, better still, the thread of the irreducible resistance. And there is no doubt that in Freud's view, this role is played by the repetition compulsion (*Wiederholungszwang*). It is the repetition compulsion—or everything that can be called by that name—that calls for working through, once the ideational, conceptual, or philosophico-theoretical resistance has been lifted, and it is once again the repetition compulsion that can always thwart the working through itself. Freud even proposes calling it simply "resistance of the unconscious."

The paradox that interests me here is that this repetition compulsion, as hyperbolic paradigm of the series, as absolute resistance, risks destroying the meaning of the series to which it is supposed to assure meaning (this is an effect of formal logic, in a certain way, as I noted a moment ago), but still more ironically, it defines no doubt a resistance that *has no meaning*—and that, moreover, is not a resistance.

I would say that what resists at this point is a nonresistance. I cannot undertake here (as I've tried to do elsewhere, in *The Post Card*) an analysis of this strange text on the "demonic" repetition compulsion, on unbinding, the death drive, and finally the analytic character—regressive, dissociative, asocial, and unbinding—of the repetition compulsion. This compulsion combines the two essential motifs of all *analysis*, the regressive or archeotropic movement and the movement of dissolution that urges toward destruction, that loves to destroy by dissociating—which is why a moment ago I called it *philolytic*. The repetition compulsion does not give its meaning to the four other forms of resistance for two reasons: it has no meaning (death drive) and it resists analysis in the form of nonresistance, for the primary reason that it is *itself of an analytic structure or vocation.* Some would be tempted to infer from this that psychoanalysis is homogeneous to it and that psychoanalytic theory, treatment, and institution represent the death drive or the repetition compulsion *at work.* This would not necessarily be a cause for complaint and it would permit one to recognize an affinity among the analytic, the demonic, and the thanatological as suggested to us by Mephistopheles and Hegel at the beginning of the session. This proposition can be turned inside out and restated intact in the following form: the repetition compulsion, hyperbolic resistance of nonresistance, is in itself *analytic*; it is that whose resistance psychoanalysis today represents, in the surest form of its ruse: disguised as nonresistance. We have here returned very close to the navel of the dream, to the place where the desire for death and desire *tout court* call for and speak the analysis they prohibit, speak it by saying nothing, respond without responding, without saying *yes* or *no*, as in "Bartleby the Scrivener." To every demand, question, pressure, request, order, it responds without responding, neither active nor passive: "I would prefer not to." Those who have read this immense little work by Melville know that Bartleby is a figure of death, to be sure, but they also know how, without saying anything, he makes others speak, above all the narrator, who happens to be a responsible man of the law and a tireless analyst. In truth incurable. Bartleby makes the analyst speak as narrator and man of the law. Bartleby is also the secret of literature. There where perhaps it makes psychoanalysis talk—or sing. "There where": the very place of resistance. Resistance of psychoanalysis—to psychoanalysis. One no longer knows who analyzes whose secret: "to death." And the man of the law mentions a rumor: some say that Bartleby used to have a subordinate responsibility at the "dead letter office" in Washington.

So I ask myself why my argument with analysis in general and with psychoanalysis in particular has always had (but this is nothing original) the deathly taste of general delivery mail [*poste restante*], which has driven me to prowl endlessly, in the company of a few others, in the vicinity of *Beyond the Pleasure Principle*.

2. The Other Secret of the Weaver

Let us change both the rhythm and the tone. When I began, I asked myself why I have always dreamed of resistance. Whether this dream had a navel. And what good there is in worrying about an *omphalos*.

When Elisabeth Rigal and Gérard Granel so generously invited me to participate in this colloquium, I answered: "I would prefer not to . . ." That certainly did not mean no; rather, it meant that, unable to prepare a real lecture in so little time (there is always so little time left) on such a large subject, on analysis, *on analysis in general*, I would try to let myself be carried along by the talk preceding me: I would try to respond to it, but in truth I was not sure of this, and I would even prefer not to have to give a response worthy of the name, which is all the more difficult after such a fine presentation. That did not prevent my friends from urging me to give a title to this nonresponse in the form of a nonlecture. Almost without thinking about it, I desired the word "resistances," exercising the basic caution of putting it in the plural so as to keep the exit doors clear. To pluralize is always to provide oneself with an emergency exit, up until the moment when it's the plural that kills you. Naturally, as I have just confirmed, although I said right away "resistances," the expression "resistance to analysis" was already governing this association. The title of the colloquium invited one to make the association. But since then I have been constantly dreaming, rather than reflecting, about the compulsion that dictated this word to me, so quickly, and I have been constantly caught up in the knot of reasons why I love it. I am going to try to explain myself schematically, very quickly, cutting short both the telling of secrets and the interminable analysis that would be de rigueur here. In other words, I am not going to tell you a story, especially not the story of how I will have heroically resisted analysis and, more radically, the Freudian analysis of analysis.

Going into reverse and breaking a movement down into its elements, I will thus propose something that could resemble an analysis. Which analysis? An analysis of the resistances to analysis, in the form in which I have been able to endure them, and the resistances to the analytic (meaning psychoanalytic) concept of analysis no less than to the philosophical (analytic or dialectical) concept of the same analysis. This makes for a bizarre procedure, I admit, just as bizarre as a failed quasi-auto-analysis, but I promise it will not last too long. What I would like to show, or in any case attest to, may be summarized as the crossing of *two entangled necessities.*

First necessity, that of a *double bind.* Every resistance supposes a tension, above all, an internal tension. Since a purely internal tension is impossible, it is a matter of an absolute inherence of the other or the outside at the heart of the internal and auto-affective tension. To take up once again the oppositions to which Miguel Giusti referred in beginning his development on Hegel, the double bind gives rise, as such, neither to an analysis nor to a synthesis, neither to an analytic nor to a dialectic. It provokes both the analytic and the dialectic to infinity, but in order to resist them *absolutely.*

Second necessity: to think this resistance as the remaining of the rest [*la restance du reste*], which is to say, in a way that is not simply ontological (neither analytic nor dialectical), since the remaining of the rest is not *psychoanalytic.* Above all because, very simply, it is not. The rest *is* not or *est* not [*Le reste n'est ou n'este pas*].

How do these two necessities intersect with each other? And what *comes about or happens* with them? Since I decided at least to mime with you, for a few minutes longer, a kind of auto-analysis that is more or less impersonal, what happened to me with these two necessities? Why am I tempted to compare what induced me into the temptation of thought—in the names of deconstruction, trace, dissemination (which could be followed by twenty or so other names that, without being synonyms, belong to the same chain)—with analysis and with this nonanalysis that one could call, for example, dialectic, even though these two are incomparable and, what is more, even though thought constantly commanded one to resist this comparison and to set out on another path? On a third path that would not be a third path and would unbind the symbolic or dialectical pact, that is, the insistent authority of the three or the third? As if what resisted the most radically and the most effectively were always the square, a last square?

What is called "deconstruction" undeniably obeys an *analytic* exigency, at once critical and analytic. It is always a matter of *undoing, desedimenting, decomposing, deconstituting* sediments, *artefacta*, presuppositions, institutions. And the insistence on unbinding, disjunction, dissociation, the being "out of joint," as Hamlet would have said, on the irreducibility of difference is so massive as to need no further insistence. Since this analytic dissociation should also in deconstruction, at least as I understand it or practice it, be a critico-genealogical return,[8] we have here apparently the two motifs of any analysis, which we have analyzed by analyzing the word *analysis*: the *archeological* or *anagogical* motif of return to the ancient as archi-originary and the *philolytic* motif of the dissociative—always very close to saying dis-social—unbinding.

But simultaneously "deconstruction" begins only with a resistance to this double motif. It even radicalizes *at the same time* its axiomatics and the critique of its axiomatics. What is put in question by its work is not only the possibility of recapturing the originary but also the desire to do so or the phantasm of doing so, the desire to rejoin the simple, whatever that may be, or the phantasm of such a reunion. At issue here is a movement of deconstruction that is not only counter-archeological but counter-genealogical: the "genealogy" of the genealogical principle no longer derives from a simple genealogy. Nothing is further from deconstruction, despite certain appearances, nothing is more foreign to it than chemistry, that science of simples with which Miguel Giusti opened his talk. What is the deconstruction of presence if not the experience of this hyperanalytic dissociation of the simple and the originary? At the heart of the present, at the origin of presence, the trace, writing, or the mark is a movement of referral to the other, to otherness, a reference as differance that would resemble an *a priori* synthesis if it were of the order of judgment and if it were thetic. But in a pre-thetic and prejudicative order, the trace is indeed an irreducible binding (*Verbindung*). Because of this originary composition, it resists a chemical type of analysis. But this binding does not bind together either presences or absences; it does not proceed either from an activity (for example, intellectual activity) or from a passivity (for example, sensory passivity). For all these reasons, it does not stem from an aesthetic, an analytic, or a transcendental dialectic. Even as it follows an argumentation that resembles, for example, the Hegelian critique of Kantian formalism and analyticism, as Miguel Giusti pointed out (when Hegel remarks that, at its most profound, Kant's procedure with regard to the *a priori* synthetic principles and their root in the unity of self-consciousness relies too much on the givens of formal logic without deducing or producing the passage of this "simple unity of self-consciousness into these determinations and differences"), the deconstructive necessity drives one to put into question even this principle of self-presence in the unity of consciousness or in this auto-determination, this logic of *Selbstbewegung*, or this immanence of the presupposition (*Voraussetzung*) that is constantly required by the Hegelian dialectic.

Basically, what resists both the Kantian analytic and its dialectical critique is still an analysis, to be sure, but it is an analysis of the presence of the present that cannot not give in to the necessity and the affirmation of a hetero-affection in the system of auto-affection and of the living present of consciousness. This is what I tried to show *by setting out from* Husserl—which is also to say by leaving him behind and taking my distance from him—a certain Husserl. Transcendental phenomenology is also an analytic of constitution—either static or genetic. The eidetic reduction and the phenomenological reduction are certainly not logical analyses, but they retain from analysis the double principle of return toward the originary and of decomposition-recomposition of an active or passive synthesis. This hetero-affection of time, which is also its originary spacing, obviously led to a displacement, following a Heideggerian movement, of the emphasis in Kantian critique. The emphasis was displaced from the analytic to the transcendental aesthetic or the theory of the schematism. Here one would have to take into account, among other things, Heidegger's regrets on this subject, my own difficulties with Heidegger on this question and a few others, and the argument deconstruction has carried on concerning analysis with each of the philosophers of the tradition, beginning with those I have just named: Kant, Hegel, Husserl, Heidegger.

Let us limit ourselves to the most formal structures of these movements. What *drives* [pousse] deconstruction to analyze without respite the analysistic and dialecticistic presuppositions of these philosophies, and no doubt of philosophy itself, what resembles there the drive and the pulse of its own movement, a rhythmic compulsion to track the desire for simple and self-present originarity, well, this very thing—here is the double bind we were talking about a moment ago—drives it to raise the analysistic and transcendentalistic stakes. It drives deconstruction to a hyperbolicism of analysis that takes sometimes, in certain people's eyes, the form of a hyperdiabolicism. In this sense, deconstruction is also the interminable drama of analysis. For in order to prevent the critique of originarism in its transcendental or ontological, analytic or dialectical form from yielding, according to the law that we well know, to empiricism or positivism, it was necessary to accede, in a still more radical, more analytic fashion, to the traditional demand, to the very law of that which had just been deconstructed: whence the impossible concepts, the quasi-concepts, the concepts that I called quasi-transcendentals, such as arche-trace or arche-writing, the arche-originary that is more "ancient" than the origin—and, above all, a donating affirmation that remains the ultimate unknown for the analysis that it nevertheless puts in motion. There is thus *announced* in this way the status without status of all the concepts and all the names of concepts—their number is nonfinite—proposed in the movement of "deconstruction." This "theory," to be sure, is called for by a thinking of writing (in *Of Grammatology*, for example) but it is better thematized and formalized (with *Dissemination, Glas, Parages*) in its relation to the *double bind*, to the *stricture of the double band* and, especially, of a *remaining* that is *not* and that does not stem from ontology any more than it lends itself to dialectical sublation. A remaining [*restance*] that, as we shall see, cannot be adequately identified with the resistance that it makes possible or that presupposes it. The place and the link—the knot—of the question that I wanted to introduce would be formed *there*. They would be formed without closing *there*. Where, there? There, in a corner wedge, unlocatable in the space of an objective topology or geometry, there, *between* remaining and resistance; in the *re-* of a repetition that, without repeating or representing anything that would be before it in space or time, without opposing itself and sometimes even without standing up in a confrontation, will have come to inscribe itself all the same like a wedge and—"before" them, between them—in the stance, estance, essence, or existence: before, that is to say, beyond the being that it institutes and destitutes at once.

This double bind, this double and unanalyzable constraint of analysis is at work on the example of all the figures called undecidable that imposed themselves under the names of *pharmakon*, supplement, hymen, differance, and a great number of others, which carried with them predicates that are contradictory or incompatible between themselves, in their very *between*, in their interlacing, their chiasmatic invagination, their *sumplokē*, or their *Geflecht*. All these figures appeared *in a series* to analysis, even as they withheld the full presence of their *as such*, announcing themselves rather than giving themselves to analysis. But each one, in its *sumplokē* and between the contradictory predicates, makes up a single trace that is not a whole, that is not identical or homogeneous to itself but that *remains*, in that very way [*en cela même*], unanalyzable.

To take only the example of the *pharmakon*, the ghost of Plato appears—it is an apparition (and all this deconstruction is also a logic of the spectral and of haunting, of surviving, neither present nor absent, alive nor dead: "I would prefer not to," and so forth)— at the end of "Plato's Pharmacy," in the guise of an analyst who would still like to separate, like chemical elements, the good rem-

edy from the bad poison, isolate them like a good repetition from a
bad repetition. In the back room of the pharmacy:

> The *analyst* [Plato is here the analyst] cocks his ears, tries to
> distinguish between two repetitions.
> He would like to isolate the good from the bad, the true from the
> false.
> He leans over further: they repeat each other.

Then, after a time, further down:

> Plato gags his ears the better to hear-himself-speak, the better to see,
> the better to analyze.
> He listens, means to distinguish, between two repetitions.
> He is searching for gold. . . .
> One ought to distinguish, between two repetitions.
> —But they repeat each other, still; they substitute for each other . . .
> —Nonsense: they don't replace each other, since they are added . . .
> —Precisely . . .⁹

It would have been necessary to insist on this concept of repetition, more precisely on the concept of iterability, which, like *itara*,
from which the word derives, says both the repetition of the same
and alteration. Why would it be strategically economical, as concerns analysis, to privilege this thematics of repetition? Once again
two reasons cross.

1. On the one hand, *iterability*, the condition of the constitution
of identities, of ideality, and, to go quickly, let's say of any concept
in general, is for this reason the becoming-objective of the object
or the becoming-subjective of the subject, thus the becoming-
analyzable in general. But (double bind), it is also what perturbs
any analysis because it perturbs, by resisting, the binary and hier-
archized oppositions that authorize any principle of distinction in
the common discourse as well as in philosophical or theoretical
discourse.¹⁰ That is why I called this iterability a quasi-concept or
an inconceivable concept. Which does not mean that iterability
authorizes confusion, approximation, or nondistinction. Whence

the reaffirmed exigency of analysis. On the contrary, iterability allows one to take into account, in the project of a new general analytic, the phenomena of anomaly, accident, the marginal, and the parasitic. Thus it also allows one to take into account what resists analysis, for example, what resists analysis as psychoanalysis.

2. For, on the other hand, if it is strategically important to point out the problem of repetition and iterability, that is because all the difficulties of the greatest resistance to analysis that we acknowledged in the first part of this lecture were leading us back finally to this resistance of resistances, in the face of which Freudian psychoanalysis found both its resource and its limit, namely, the repetition compulsion. To put into a sentence what would require a long discourse: there is nothing fortuitous about the fact that the most decisive and difficult stakes between, let's say, "psychoanalysis" and "deconstruction" should have taken a relatively organized form around the question of the repetition compulsion. The great reference texts here are *Beyond the Pleasure Principle* and Lacan's "Seminar on 'The Purloined Letter,' " which explicitly takes its point of departure in this text by Freud. Since it is out of the question for me to open once again, even for a second, the dossier of the argument I have attempted elsewhere with these two texts (in *The Post Card*, in particular), I will simply point out two possible entries, from our viewpoint this evening, namely, analysis.

First entry: the reading I proposed of *Beyond the Pleasure Principle*, a book that begins, as did Miguel Giusti's lecture, with the apparition of Mephistopheles and that turns speech over, so to speak, to the *advocatus diaboli* of the death drive. This reading tends to acknowledge, in the paradoxes of *Bindung* (binding, linking) and of "solution" or "extinction" (*Erlöschung*), the very thing that endlessly sets the analysis and the thesis going again, beyond any *Aufhebung*, any *Setzung*, and any analytic *position*.[11] There is no analytic position once resistance is not identifiable. As for the analytic position, it can only be a resistance to this law. From this point of view, as I recalled at the beginning of "To Speculate on—'Freud,' " it is then a matter of a putting to work and at the same time of a putting into question the principle of analysis, since *The Post Card* is, like *Glas,* a book on the bind (*Band*), the *nexum,* the *desmos,* or the stricture, and on a certain "unsolvable—postal effect."[12]

Second entry: In the argument with the "Seminar on the 'Purloined Letter,' " one of the most strategically decisive places (which are perhaps decisive because they forbid decision and thereby assign it its place: one only decides there where it is impossible), would still be this letter, which Lacan says does not bear partition. By contesting this thesis, which I hold to be dogmatic and idealist, by giving the counter-demonstration that the letter is divisible, I was recalling in effect a principle of interminable analysis: an axiom of interminability, perhaps. Because dissociability is always possible (and with it the undoing of the social bond, dissociability), because one must always and can always analyze, divide, differentiate further, because the philolytic principle of analysis is invincible, one cannot assemble anything whatsoever in its indivisibility. The archeological or anagogical principle of analysis is always destined to failure. And if one does not like the word "failure," which is no doubt not the best one, since a chance in the falling-due and a given of the fall are also involved, let us say that this principle is destined to the limit of its arrest or to the finitude of its suspense, there where it can no longer *touch* what it claims to be aiming at and therefore begins or ends up by losing its *pertinence.*

The possibility of unbinding is also, of course, the only condition of possibility for binding in general. This tension between the *archeological* principle and the *philolytic* principle of analysis could be substituted for the duality of the Freudian principles in *Beyond the Pleasure Principle.* The question of divisibility is one of the most powerful instruments of formalization for what is called deconstruction. If, in an absurd hypothesis, there were one and only one deconstruction, a sole *thesis* of "Deconstruction," it would pose divisibility: differance as divisibility. Paradoxically, this amounts to raising the analytical stakes for a thinking that is very careful to take account of what always rejects analysis (the originary complication, the nonsimple, the origin under erasure, the trace, or the affirmation of the gift as trace). This paradox is merely apparent: it is because there is no indivisible element or simple origin that analysis is interminable. Divisibility, dissociability, and thus the impossibility of arresting an analysis, like the necessity of thinking the possibility of this indefiniteness, would be perhaps, if one insisted on such a thing, the truth without truth of deconstruction, at least the one that is de-marcated both from the "spiritual bond" (*das geistige Band*) of the Goethian-Hegelian Mephistopheles, which Miguel Giusti evoked for us at the beginning of this session, and from the Heideggerian *Versammlung*, from that always ultimate reassembling of the same in which, for Heidegger, all difference is gathered up: the one, Being, the *logos*, the *polemos*—and *Geist*.

One cannot separate this divisibility of the letter, of course, from the force of unbinding (another analytic phenomenon), which undoes the link, for example, the link of the debt, the symbolic, the name of the father. These are all motifs that link and are linked to the triangle or the circle of reappropriation whose trinitary figures dominate the "Seminar on the 'Purloined Letter.' " They give it the firm consistency of an exceptionally well-organized resistance, as does its affirmation that a letter always arrives at its destination. This is one of the places of division between the three and the four, between the resistance bound up in all repressions and the disseminal remaining that not only *does not come back to the father*, as I tried to demonstrate,[13] but is exposed to a radical forgetting that no longer belongs to the topic or the economy of repression, destined as it is to chance and to ashes, namely, to a trace without trace: inviolable secret, without depth, without place, without name, without destination, *hyperbolytic*, excessive destruction, and lysis without measure, without measure and *without return*, lysis without anagogy.

Here I must cut things off and conclude somewhat abruptly. I conclude with the cut, precisely, and the paradox of decision concerning analysis. What we have just approached is *both* a hyperanalytic necessity—the law of a "one must analyze endlessly," what is more, "it is analyzing itself indefinitely," "it is indefinitely analyzable," therefore it must be analyzed hyperbolytically, *there remains* always to be analyzed—*and as well* the other law that enjoins us to take into account what is more or less than a resistance to analysis, a remaining of this "there remains to" that makes of every analytic *telos* (the term of the analysis as principial of the principle, of the simple element, of the originary, or the *arkhē*) another resistance to analysis. In both cases, reason is at stake—and the decision concerning reason, including Enlightenment Reason in its obedience to the Principle of reason. What is called *Aufklärung*, Enlightenment, or, in the difference of its French version, *l'époque des Lumières*, is also a certain nonmathematical analyticism (not always simply Cartesian): from Locke to the French Ideologues, from Rousseau to Condillac, as from Hume to Kant, it is the concern to render reason from meaning by posing questions about the origin, by returning to the elementary, by breaking things down and deriving.

The hyperanalyticism with which I identify "deconstruction" is a double gesture in this regard, double and contradictory, doubly bound, which is to say, bound/unbound in what one can call a double bind or double constraint:

1. *on the one hand*, to inherit and take inspiration from this Enlightenment, as from that which is repeated, reaffirmed, and displaced in our time—within both the reason of a transcendental phenomenology as well as within psychoanalytic reason and even, despite his lack of sympathy or apparent affinity with *Aufklärung*, within the existential analytic of the *Dasein* and the whole path of thinking thereby opened by Heidegger;

2. *on the other hand*, to analyze tirelessly the resistance that still clings to the thematic of the simple and the indivisible origin, to oppositional logic—which dialectic does not put into question— and to all that which, by repeating the origin, attempts constantly to reappropriate, restitute, or reconstitute the social bond, most often, whether one declares it or denies it, by renaturalizing it. What I have tried to analyze, in both Lacan (in *The Post Card*) and Heidegger (in *The Truth in Painting*) on the subject of *restitution* and the reconstitution of the symbolic pact, stems from this axiomatics.

The paradox, in which one neither can nor should *set oneself up*, for one does not set oneself up in a paradox, the law of this antinomy, which can only be endured in its tension (and all antinomies, those of Kant in particular, are the fated outcomes of analysis), is thus the paradox of a double "one must": "one must," to be sure, analyze the "one must" of analytic desire as the desire to undo a composition or an originary contamination so as finally to attain a primitive, proper, or elementary simplicity that would be by rights the sole and true point of departure, the sole legitimate beginning, which Miguel Guisti spoke of earlier. These are other names for pure life or pure death: for me, it's the same thing and everything I say goes as much against a philosophy of life as against its simple contrary. But here, without delay, comes the double bind: to analyze such a desire does not mean to renounce its law and to suspend the order of reason, of meaning, of the question of the origin, of the social bond. One must equally take into account, so as to render an account of, the archeo-logical, anagogical, and also hermeneutic demand of reason and the principle of reason: as concerns meaning, resistance, repression, conflict of forces, and so forth.

Is not this *double bind* (a term I leave in English because it names the bind, that is, the call to *analysis*, which is not the case with the French expression *double contrainte* that is sometimes used to translate it) the question of analysis itself? Not that one must *assume* the double bind. By definition a double bind cannot be assumed; one can only endure it in *passion*. Likewise, a double bind cannot be fully analyzed: one can only unbind one of its knots by pulling on the other to make it tighter, in the movement I have called *stricture*.[14]

But if a double bind cannot be assumed, there are several ways of enduring it. First, by ceasing to believe it is merely a classifiable and circumscribable pathology, which is what we are sometimes urged to believe when, beginning with Bateson and others, it is assigned a schizogenic power to which some fall victim while others are immune. I will not venture to argue that the double bind is never "pathological" (in the terribly trivial and "real" meaning of this word) and reveals only a transcendental illness of the analytic or the hyperbolytic as such. But it is an illness that is no more fortuitous or pathological than all the pathetic figures of death. Next, if a double bind cannot be assumed but is endured in a thousand different ways, if all passions are irreplaceably assigned to singularity, if a double bind is never one and general but is the infinitely divisible dissemination of knots, of thousands and thousands of knots of passion, this is because without it, without this double bind and without the ordeal of aporia that it determines, there would only be programs or causalities, not even fated necessities, and no decision would ever take place. No responsibility, I will go so far as to say no event would take place. Not even analysis. Not even the place.

Let us tie up the threads again, so as to fall back into the web or the net that Miguel Guisti has just set for me. I would have liked to convince you that by going from three to four, from two to endless and bottomless divisibility, I have merely allowed to resonate what was in fact, in deed and at the beginning (*Im Anfang war die Tat!*), the Mephistophelic word. This word also announced a certain delay, the latecomer philosopher.

> Zwar ist's mit der Gedankenfabrik
> Wie mit einem Weber-Meisterstück,
> Wo ein Tritt tausend Fäden regt,
> Die Schifflein herüber hinüber schiessen,
> Die Fäden ungesehen fliessen,
> Ein Schlag tausend Verbindungen schlägt:
> Der Philosoph, der tritt herein
> Und beweist Euch, es muss'so sein:
> Das Erst'wär'so, das Zweite so,
> Und drum das Dritt' und Vierte so,
> Und wenn das Erst' und Zweit' nicht wär,
> Das Dritt' und Viert' wär' nimmermehr

To translate: It is a fact that the making of thoughts is like a weaver's loom, where a treadle lifts thousands of threads, where the shuttle flies back and forth without stopping; then enters the philosopher [this is the delay of the philosopher, of the latecomer who analyzes after the fact and whose students will never learn the secret of how to become a weaver or, for that matter, by definition and because of an essential allergy, any other secret] and demonstrates that this is how it must be: the first is this, the second is that, therefore the third and the fourth are that; and if the first and the second did not exist, the third and the fourth would not exist either. Students from every land think highly of this reasoning and yet not one of them has become a weaver.

> Das preisen die Schüler aller Orten
> Sind aber keine Weber geworden.

§ 2 For the Love of Lacan

1. The Future Anterior in the Conditional

What wouldn't Lacan have said!

What will he not have said!

This is an exclamation rather than a question: I am trying out my voice, looking for the right tone, as in an experiment prior to beginning this idiomatic conjunction of negation, disavowal, the conditional, and the future anterior. My hypothesis: these grammars play either successively or simultaneously a role of screen and mirror in the modalities of the *with* [avec]. As well as in the modalities of the *since* [depuis], which will have determined Lacan's relation to the philosophers—to certain philosophers. These brief observations on temporal modalities will all be marked by the incidence of Stephen Melville's observations (see headnote, p. 121) on "narration," thus on history, on the "temporal shifts," and also on the possibility of a *Kehre*, a "turning point" in Lacan following the *Ecrits*, that is, more precisely, since 1966–67.

What will Lacan not have said! What wouldn't he have said!

What was it with Lacan *with* the philosophers? To approach this question, it would be necessary to shed light not only on what "with" can mean in this case, but on what Lacan said, did not say, will have or will not have said, caused to be said, or let be said—in the future anterior or in the conditional. To deal with this enigma of the future anterior and the conditional, which is what I will be

39

particularly interested in today, is to deal with the problem of archivization, of what remains or does not remain. It is an old, familiar problem. During this century, however, the birth of psychoanalysis, in *conjunction* with the advent of new techniques of archivization or telecommunication, has consolidated the apparatus of certain paradoxes with which, in my view at least, conventional history, the way in which history or histories are written or told, has not yet systematically come to terms. Quite simply, the concept of history is no doubt at stake. The effects of these paradoxes, which could be termed techno-psychoanalytical (since they concern, *conjointly* and by the same token, what psychoanalysis can tell us about inscription, erasure, blanks, the non-said, memory storage, *and* new techniques of archivization—this one, for example—look at all the tape recorders that are in this room), do not exclusively concern Lacan, of course. But the example of Lacan offers certain singular aspects that merit the attention of anyone interested in these questions.

One problem with colloquia, a problem I at least find hard to bear, is that no one goes into details. Instead of treating "things themselves" (ah, things themselves!) with as keen an eye as possible, we must, for lack of time and because our voice is swept along by swelling, choruslike rhythms, make do without the minutiae of the letter, that is, those microscopic or micrological displacements where I incorrigibly persist in hoping things get decided—at a given moment. But the given moment is never given. That this given moment be given is just what is never given in advance, and here we have arrived, too soon, of course, well in advance, at the question of destination.

Owing to this macroscopia or macrologic of the colloquium, movements of "external" strategy—if one can put it that way and if there were a purely external strategy, which I do not believe—tend in the main to prevail. What thus tends to prevail are theses, positions, position takings, positionings. I've never much liked these things, and I've rarely stopped to consider theses, which is not only a question of taste. It is nothing less than the question of philosophy, of what is accorded there to the *thesis*, to *positionality*.

In a reading of *Beyond the Pleasure Principle*, which is not just any book by Freud and, as you know, not just any book by Freud for Lacan, I attempted (in "To Speculate—on 'Freud' ") to indicate in what way Freud advanced only by suspending, without any possibility of stopping, all the theses at which his successors or heirs, his readers in general, would have liked to see him stop. That reading was also an interpretation of what links speculation on the name, the proper name, or family names to science, particularly to the theory and the institution of psychoanalysis. It goes without saying that my reading also concerned, explicitly (provided that a certain code or program of translation was available), the question of Lacan's name, the problems of legacy, of science and institution, and the aporias of archivization in which that name is involved.

I will thus attempt to resist once more the impulse toward or expectation of position taking. To those who are waiting for me to take a position so they can reach a decision [*arrêter leur jugement*], I say, "Good luck."

So as not to become lost in the quantity and difficulty of the problems that would have to be addressed, so as not to keep you here too long, so as not to reopen all the texts, which are, after all, available to and in principle legible by whoever wants to look at them, I will take as my rule discussion (since this is the time for discussion), above all the discussion as it has been initiated by René Major and Stephen Melville in what they have just said. But it goes without saying that, following my remarks, it will be up to you to propose, if you wish, another space for this discussion.

René Major cited the incipit of Lacan's seminar of November 16, 1976, which begins "Were you able to read the poster? [*Avez-vous su lire l'affiche?*]," and which speaks of the *insuccès*, the nonsuccess ("l'Insu-que-sait," the "Unknown-known"). I translate this in my own manner (which is perhaps already no longer very Lacanian) as "l'insuccès qui échoue *à* arriver," "the nonsuccess that fails *to* arrive," which is to say, the failure that fails—because it arrives, because it succeeds, that fails *to* succeed. (The syntax of "to" displaces itself here surreptitiously, but very necessarily, and I have often played on this, in order to pass from one grammar to another:

"I fail to arrive" means at the same time "I do not arrive," "I do not arrive at arriving," *and* I fail or I do not arrive *because* I arrive, I do not arrive *at* arriving, *once, because, since* I arrive—here it is the event that speaks, it is of the event, the arrival, the coming, and the "come" that I am speaking.) Speaking, then, of the "insuccès" as what does not succeed in arriving, precisely *by* arriving, by the fact of arriving, because it arrives, Major cites Lacan's seminar dated November 16, 1976: "The single stroke [*le trait unaire*] interests us because, as Freud points out, it does not necessarily have to do with a loved one."[1] Major is quite right to add: "I hasten to add that it is not always those who love you who render you the greatest service."

I would be dead if I didn't believe he was right on this point. I would be dead and, if I have understood correctly, this would not be without some secondary benefit, at least for my name; but I preferred to let things wait.

And if I were to say now: "You see, I think that we loved each other very much, Lacan and I," I am almost certain that many of you here would not stand for it. Many would not stand for it, which explains a lot of things. Many would not stand for it, and not because it surprised them, not at all; I even wonder if this idea is not strangely familiar to them. Not because of surprise, then, but because it is a thing that ought not to have happened and above all that cannot be said without presumptuousness, especially by a sole speaker who says "we" all alone after the death of the other. Thus the Thing should not be said and especially not repeated; and yet, if I repeated "we loved each other very much, Lacan and I, each as he will have pleased, each in his way or each in our way," would that constitute a revelation, a confession, or a denunciation? Let everyone take this "as it may please him."

This "as it may please him" is a quotation from Lacan, from a quasi-private phrase between Lacan and myself, in which "him" is me. I will return to this shortly.

As for being shocked to hear someone say "we" when speaking all alone after the death of the other, there is no reason for it. This is one of the most common phenomena of what I have called *destinerrance*. It inflicts an internal drift on the destination of the letter, from which it may never return, but to which we will have to return.

"We" is a modality of the *with*, of the being-with or the doing-with: *avoc, apud hoc*, at the home of [*chez*] the other, as guest or parasite. "We" is always said by a sole person. It is always a sole person who has the gall to say "we psychoanalysts," "we philosophers," "with you psychoanalysts," "with us philosophers," or, still more seriously, "we psychoanalysts with the philosophers" or "with us philosophers." "Avec" (with) also means "chez" (at the home of; *apud, avuec, avoc, apud hoc,* category of the guest or the intruder, of the host or the parasite, therefore, who always takes advantage as soon as he says "we").

This logico-grammatical modality seems interesting because, among other things, it is always me who says "we"; it is always an "I" who utters "we," supposing thereby, in effect, in the asymmetrical structure of the utterance, the other to be absent, dead, in any case incompetent, or even arriving too late to object.

The one signs for the other.

The asymmetry is even more violent if we're talking about a reflexive, reciprocal, or specular "we." Who will ever have the right to say: "We love each other"? But is there any other origin of love, any other amorous performative than this presumptuousness? If there is some "we" in being-with, it is because there is always one who speaks all alone in the name of the other, from the other; there is always one of them who lives more, lives longer. I will not hasten to call this one the "subject." When we are with someone, we know *without delay* that one of us will survive the other. So he already does and will be able or will have to speak on his own. And one can immediately draw the consequences from this. This happens every day. Even when we are singing the "Marseillaise" or joining in a chorus, what remains the exception and does not commit us very much is a self that can say "we," for example, "we love each other."

What is getting archived!

That is not a question. It is once again an exclamation, with a somewhat suspended exclamation point because it is always difficult to know if it is getting archived, what is getting archived, how it is getting archived—the trace that arrives only to efface itself / only by effacing itself, beyond the alternative of presence and absence. It is not merely difficult to know this; it is strictly impossible, no doubt not because there is always more to be known but because it is not of the order of knowledge.

This is never a sufficient reason not to seek to know, as an *Aufklärer*—to know that it is getting archived, within what limits, and how, according to what detoured, surprising, or overdetermined paths. Earlier, René Major alluded first to an "underground" history in the trajectory of Lacan's discourse and then to a "question in question" that, I quote, "has a history, concerns texts, several texts, which are neither limited to an identifiable circle nor delimited by a geographic area, and this despite the fact that—even if and especially if—it does not take the advertised form of an academic and institutional program. The question of the question is more vast and stems from procedures of translation and theoretico-practical issues that join up at the borders (of several disciplines) that they destabilize."[2]

Yes, I believe that this is true in general and more particularly for what is in question under the title "Lacan with the Philosophers." The modalities of the "with" here call for a history and a type of historical interpretation that would have to be extremely careful and slow, bringing to bear great micrological refinement; they call for constant attention to the paradoxes of archivization, to what psychoanalysis (which would not be just the theme or the object of this history but its interpretation) can tell us about these paradoxes of archivization, about its blanks, the efficacy of its details or its nonappearance, its capitalizing reserve or—but here we perhaps step beyond psychoanalysis—about the radical destruction of the archive, in ashes, without the repression and the putting in reserve or on guard that would operate in repression through a mere topical displacement. An equally keen attention is required with regard to what may be problematic in psychoanalytic discourse— for example, Lacan's—as concerns, precisely, archivization, the guard or reserve, the economy of repression as guard, inscription, effacement, the destructibility of the letter or the name. A history that could measure up to these formidable difficulties, could be capable of taking them into account in its own historical discourse, ought to come as an addition to other readings of the archive— whether conventional or not, and more classically symptomatic— without in the least disqualifying them, since they are just as indispensable or at least inevitable. This is not about to happen soon.

Before proposing, in response to what has just been said, a modest, partial, and preliminary contribution to such a history, I will explain in a few words why and in what spirit I accepted the invitation so graciously extended by my friends at the Collège International de Philosophie, René Major and Patrick Guyomard—who, I believe, first had the fine idea of this plural and international colloquium. If I said "yes," it is certainly not because I think I had something more or irreplaceable to say on these matters; the discussion of what I ventured almost twenty years ago around these questions would demand a microscopic examination for which neither you nor I have the time or the patience; as I've already said, such an examination is, moreover, ill suited to the rhythm and setting of a large colloquium. No, if I was happy to accept the invitation—and if I did so almost two years ago, even before I knew who would be speaking here and what would be said, in particular what Major would say, or even what would be the title of his talk, since it never occurred to me to ask him—it is because this colloquium (besides the considerable and necessary work that can go on here on subjects that have been too often avoided up to now, especially within the analytic milieu, including the milieu around Lacan) also constitutes an international homage to Lacan. And it is with this event, this justly deserved and spectacular homage to Lacan, that I was happy to be asked to associate myself. Not only but also because, in our time—and I mean the time of culture and especially Parisian culture—I find a political significance in this homage. I consider it an act of cultural resistance to pay homage publicly to a difficult form of thought, discourse, or writing, one which does not submit easily to normalization by the media, by academics, or by publishers, one which rebels against the restoration currently underway, against the philosophical or theo-

retical neo-conformism in general (let us not even mention literature) that flattens and levels everything around us, in the attempt to
make one forget what the Lacan era was, along with the future and
the promise of his thought, thereby erasing the *name* of Lacan. As
you know, there are countless ways to do this, sometimes very
paradoxical ways; in his lifetime, Lacan underwent the experience
dubbed "excommunication." Some of those who claim to draw on
Lacan's name, and not just his legacy, can be not the least active or
the least effective in this operation. Here, once again, the logic of
the "service rendered" is highly tricky, and censorship, suturing,
and defense of orthodoxy do not in the least exclude—quite the
contrary—a facade of cultural eclecticism. Whether one is talking
about philosophy, psychoanalysis, or theory in general, what the
flat-footed restoration underway attempts to recover, disavow, or
censor is the fact that nothing of that which managed to transform
the space of thought in the last decades would have been possible
without some coming to terms *with* Lacan, without the Lacanian
provocation, however one receives it or discusses it—and, I will
add, without some coming to terms *with* Lacan in his coming to
terms *with* the philosophers.

With the philosophers rather than with philosophy: I have
always been seduced by the dramatization in which Lacan broke
with the commentary or the historiography in use by many professional philosophers either when they give a more or less competent
account of philosophers' lives or when they reconstitute the structure of systems. Instead, he staged the singular desire *of the* philosopher and thereby contributed considerably to opening the space for
a sort of new philosophical culture. In which we are situated,
despite efforts to make us forget it so as to turn back the clock. In
Lacan, the being-with or the coming-to-terms-with the philosophers attained a refinement, a scope, an unexpected illumination of
the "searchlight effect" [*"coup de phare"*] of which there are few
other examples either in the community of professional philosophers or in that of psychoanalysts. Therefore rarely to this degree
will a frequenting of philosophers, a being-with philosophers,
have—and I say this in the sense of the greatest favor or fervor—

merited discussion, merited that one discuss *with* Lacan the manner
in which he will have managed his relations *with* the philosophers.
Lacan's refinement and competence, his philosophical originality,
have no precedent in the tradition of psychoanalysis. The return to
a Freud-philosopher would have been from this point of view a
regression or a weakness. Later on I will say a brief word about the
paradoxical and perverse consequences that flow from the fact that
Lacan is so much more aware as a philosopher than Freud, so much
more a philosopher than Freud!

Having thus accepted with pleasure the invitation to participate
in this reflection, this discussion, and this homage, I did not think I
ought to take offense or become discouraged, as others might
legitimately have done, and as some perhaps wished I would do,
when they put forward the pretext of a rule according to which
only the dead could be spoken about here and therefore, if one
insisted on speaking of me, one could do so only under the
condition that I play dead, even before the fact, and that I be given
a helping hand when the occasion arose.[3] That is (it was enough
just to think of it) to make me disappear nominally as a live
person—because I am alive—to make me disappear *for* life. So I
thought I should not let myself get offended or discouraged, bon
vivant that I still am, by the lamentable and indecent incident of
the barring of my proper name from the program billing [*af-
fichage*], of the veto exercised against those remains of a proper
name that may be an adjective or attribute. I am referring to the
"acting out" to which Major alluded a moment ago and whose
essentials he in fact summarized. Although I was indeed shocked,
as were many, by the symptomatic and compulsive violence of that
acting out, I was not surprised by what it symptomized, for I have
had a lot of practice analyzing this symptom for almost a quarter of
a century. Therefore, to save time, I will not add anything more for
the moment—because I find all this increasingly tedious and because, let's say, "I know only too well." There is, finally, another
reason: even if one sets aside the sinister political memory we have
of the history that, in France and especially in eastern France, has
been written, so to speak, not in ink but in the effacement of the

name, even, then, if one sets aside this political memory, the most
important of what there is to say on this subject has been said, by
none other than Freud and by Lacan—who knew what he was
talking about. And, if I may be allowed this self-reference, elsewhere, in several books, including one on the names of Freud and
Lacan, I have already sufficiently formalized readability under
erasure and the logic of the event as graphematic event—notably as
event of the proper name, in which the little devil arrives only to
erase itself / by erasing itself—to be spared having to add anything
here for the moment. It is advisable out of modesty at least to
follow such a course, since in this case it seems to be a matter of my
so-called proper name or of what may remain of it in an epithet.
That said, if any among you wish me to do so, I will not insist on
silencing what I think of all this, but only at the end, after we're
done, as a post-scriptum, in parentheses, or "off the record" as one
says in English.

"Off the record" means not recorded, outside the archive. We are
thus brought back to the difficult question of the record, history,
and the archive. Is there an "outside-the-archive"? Impossible, but
the impossible is deconstruction's affair.

At bottom, beneath the question that I will call once again the
remaining [*restance*] of the archive—which does anything but *remain* in the sense of the permanent subsistence of a presence—
beneath this question of the differance or the destinerrance of the
archive, there could take shape, at least for the time of a session, the
silhouette of everything that, in my view, deserves to be discussed,
since we are here to discuss or to continue discussions. By this I
mean the silhouette of what seemed to me to deserve discussion not
with Lacan *in general* and certainly not in the name of philosophy
in general (on the subject, in the name, or from the point of view of
which I have never spoken, no more than of antiphilosophy, as a
consequence, which has always seemed to me the thing least
deserving of interest in the world). Thus, not *with* Lacan *in general*—who for me does not exist, and I never speak of a philosopher
or a corpus in general as if it were a matter of a homogeneous body:
I did not do so for Lacan any more than for any other. The dis-

cussion was begun rather with a forceful, relatively coherent, and stabilized configuration of a discourse at the time of the collection and binding of *Ecrits*, in other words, in 1966.

The binding of *Ecrits* is what holds it together and provides it with the most solid, systematic structure, the most formalized constructure, as formalized as possible. Now if there is one text that stands more than any other in this position and at this post of binder, it is the "Seminar on 'The Purloined Letter.' " As you know, the "Seminar on 'The Purloined Letter' " is given a "privilege," which is Lacan's word; I quote Lacan: "the privilege of opening the sequence [the sequence of *Ecrits*] despite its diachrony."[4] In other words, *Ecrits* collects and binds together all the texts out of which it is composed in the chronological order (according to the "diachrony") of their prior publication, with the exception of the "Seminar on 'The Purloined Letter,' " which, by coming at the beginning, is thereby given the "privilege" of figuring the synchronic configuration of the set and thus *binding* the whole together. It therefore seemed to me legitimate to take a privileged interest in this privilege. If I use the word *binding* here, the binding that holds together at the moment of reading and rereading, it is because on one of the two sole occasions in my life on which I met Lacan and spoke briefly *with* him, he himself spoke to me of binding and of the binding of *Ecrits*. I am not telling these stories for the sake of the amusement or distraction of anecdotes, but because what we are supposed to be talking about here is the encounter, *tukhē*, contingency—or not—and what binds, if you will, the signature of the event to the theorem.

I only met Lacan twice, though I crossed paths with him a third time, long after, at a cocktail party. I don't know if that means we were together, one *with* the other, but in any case these two encounters did not take place at the home of (*apud*) one or the other but at a third party's, first abroad, in 1966 in the United States, to which both of us had been for the first time exported. (I say "exported" on purpose. In fact it is a quotation; perhaps you know that behind the pseudonyms deemed to be transparent by the newspapers, the recognizable character from a very bad novel [when I say bad, I mean in the "literary" sense and not only the "moral" sense]—who complains about not being translated abroad, complaining with a bitterness that seems to permeate the very paper on which it is written—said quite recently, in a single breath, that Lacan and I, Lacan *with* me, alias Lauzun *with* Saïda for those in the know, were both of us "adulterated products fit for exportation." To find myself in the same export container with Lacan would have been rather to my taste, but this was not bearable for everyone or to everyone's taste, since a journalist who shuttles back and forth between the editorial board of Gallimard and *Le Nouvel Observateur* attempted to separate me *from* [d'avec] Lacan by saying that, for the author of this disconcerting novel, it was only Derrida—using my name, not that of the fictional character, not even Saïd, Sida, or Saïda—who, this time in the singular, through an adulterated quotation, becomes an "adulterated product fit for exportation." I alone, no longer *with* Lacan, as the author or the character of the fable wanted it, but without Lacan, me all alone now, "adulterated product" in the export container, me all alone in my box, deported, exported abroad, and, why not, forbidden to frequent certain places, forbidden a resident's permit, me all alone, isolated, insulated by the decree of a cultural traffic cop. This is one of the things that is happening in France today, in the higher spheres of culture and politics that I spoke of at the outset.)[5]

So, to start over, when I met Lacan in Baltimore for the first time, in 1966—we were introduced to each other by René Girard—his first words, uttered in a friendly sigh, were: "So we had to wait to come here, and abroad, in order to meet each other!" Here, I remark, perhaps because of the problem of destinerrance that is waiting for us and perhaps because of Baltimore's mortal name (Baltimore: dance or trance and terror), Baltimore the city of Poe, whose grave I looked for in vain during those days, although I was able to visit his house on that occasion (I went *chez* Poe in 1966), perhaps then because of this mortal name of Baltimore, I remark that the only two times we met and spoke briefly one *with* the other, it was a question of death between us, and first of all from Lacan's mouth. In Baltimore, for example, he spoke to me of the way in which he thought he would be read, in particular by me, after his death.

At our second and last encounter, during a dinner offered by his in-laws, he insisted on publicly archiving in his own way, with regard to something I had told him, the disregard of the Other that I had supposedly attempted "by playing dead." Elisabeth Roudinesco recounts very well this whole episode, which I reread this morning on page 418 of her monumental and classic *History of Psychoanalysis in France* (volume 2). Lacan's phrase speaks of a "father," and that's me, a father who "does not recognize . . . the way he himself disregarded the Other [big O] by playing dead."[6] I am still not sure I have fully understood the ventured interpretation in what was, we should not forget, a signed publication in *Scilicet* (where Lacan alone was authorized, by himself, to sign), but I have always wondered whether by making me out to be the father in this story, by naming me "the father," he was not taking aim at the son; I have always wondered whether he didn't mean to say the son, if he didn't want to play the son, to make me or himself into the son, to make of me the son who disregards the Other by playing dead, as he put it, or make himself into the son. As always, Lacan left me the greatest freedom of interpretation, and as always I would have taken it even if he had not left it to me, as it will have pleased me. He left me the greatest freedom to hear and to interpret because he added right after this: "To the father who said it to me, from here to hear me or not [*Au père qui me l'a dit d'ici m'entendre ou non*]." (This *didici* is magnificent; I hear it in Latin, as if in the dark of a disco this time, and not a ballroom, of a disco where the old professor cannot manage to give up [*n'arrive pas à renoncer*] the combined compulsion of the future anterior and didactics: *didici*, I will have told you, I will have taught you.) Lacan left me this freedom to interpret as I please on the flyleaf of *Ecrits* when it was bound, because the dedication that accompanies it says: "to Jacques Derrida, this homage to take as it may please him." Message received: I have always, and again today, used this homage as it pleases me and as it pleases me to give it and to give it back [*le rendre*].

So there was death between us; it was especially a question of death, I will say even *only* of the death of one of us, as it is *with* or *chez* all those who love each other. Or rather he spoke about it, he alone, since for my part I never breathed a word about it. He spoke, alone, about our death, about his death that would not fail to arrive, and about the death or rather the dead one that, according to him, I was playing.

I am not forgetting the binding with which all of this is bound up. The other worry Lacan confided to me in Baltimore concerned the binding of *Ecrits*, which had not yet appeared, although its publication was imminent. Lacan was worried and slightly annoyed, it seemed to me, with those at Le Seuil, his publishers, who had advised him to assemble everything in a single large volume of more than nine hundred pages. There was thus a risk that the binding would not be strong enough and would give way: "You'll see," he told me as he made a gesture with his hands, "it's not going to hold up." The republication in the two-volume paperback edition in 1970 will thus have reassured him and will have allowed him, in passing, not only to confirm the necessity of placing the "Seminar on 'The Purloined Letter'" at the "entry post" of *Ecrits*, but also to fire off one of those future anteriors (antedates or antidotes) that will have been the privileged mode of all the declarations of love that he so often made to me, by mentioning (I dare not say by antedating), and I quote, "what I call literally the instance of the letter prior to any grammatology."[7]

(Prior to any grammatology: "Of Grammatology" was first the title of an article published some five years before Lacan's new introduction and—this is one of the numerous mistakes or misrecognitions made by Lacan and so many others—it never proposed a grammatology, some positive science or discipline bearing that name;[8] on the contrary, both the article and later the book of the same title went to great lengths to demonstrate the impossibility, the conditions of impossibility, the absurdity, in principle, of any science or any philosophy bearing the name "grammatology." The book that treated *of grammatology* was anything but a grammatology.)

I link this and bind it once again to the binding of the great book. I go back then to the period (the end of the 1960s, 1965, 1966–67) when *Ecrits* was being bound under the sign of the "Seminar on 'The Purloined Letter.'" I would now like to venture a modest contribution to this history to come of the *being-with* of Lacan and the philosophers, a history which I am quite sure has never been written and which I am not sure ever can be written, even assuming it can be deciphered. What I will propose, then, are merely a few protocols for such a history, whether or not it is possible. And since I have already spoken too long, I will limit myself somewhat arbitrarily to *three protocols*. I am certain there is enough psychoanalysis and psychoanalysts here to prevent anyone from dismissing as self-indulgence or coquetry the fact that I will describe things not from an overview looking down on this history from above, but necessarily from the place where I was and am still situated, inscribed, engaged, invested. A place that, I must say, will not have been very comfortable but also not a bad one for observation. I will schematize the three protocols according to several figures under the following headings:

1. *chiasmus*
2. *the future anterior of the after-the-fact* [l'après-coup]
3. *chiasmatic invagination of the borders—or the site of analysis*

What happens to the *with between two* when there is chiasmus, the after-the-fact of the future anterior, and chiasmatic invagination?

2. First Protocol: Chiasmus

Chiasmus was mentioned by Major. He spoke of the chiasmus between the trajectories of Freud and Lacan as regards science and philosophical speculation. I would like to give the example of another chiasmus that occurs in France during the 1960s. When the "Seminar on 'The Purloined Letter'" proposes the broadest strategic formalization of the Lacanian discourse at the opening of *Ecrits*, what is happening with the philosophers? Here we can no longer speak—assuming that we ever could—of philosophers *in general*, but of what happens to some of them, or of what happens to philosophy through some of them who are perhaps no longer simply philosophers, without having anything against philosophy, which would be rather simplistic and scholastic. It so happened— and it happened to me—that at the moment when a certain number of major or dominant philosophers, organized into what I proposed at the time naming phonocentrism and/or phallogo-centrism, called for (so to speak, to go quickly) a deconstructive questioning (a questioning that was obviously, by definition, both philosophical and eccentric, ex-centering in relation to the philo-sophical as such, giving one to think the philosophical from a place that could no longer be simply philosophical or counter-philosophical, within or outside philosophy), at the same moment, exactly the same moment, it was possible to witness a theoretical binding of the Lacanian discourse that made the most strenuous, and powerfully spectacular, use of all the motifs that were in my view deconstructible, undergoing deconstruction. Even more se-rious, in my opinion, was the fact that it concerned not only the most deconstructible motifs of philosophy (phonocentrism, logo-centrism, phallogocentrism, full speech as truth, the transcenden-talism of the signifier, the circular return of reappropriation toward what is most proper about the proper place, whose borders are circumscribed by lack, and so forth, through a handling of philo-sophical reference whose form, at least, was in the best of cases elliptical and aphoristic, in the worst, dogmatic—I will come back to this in a moment) but even that which, crossing through and overflowing philosophy or onto-theology (I mean the Heideg-gerian discourse), seemed to me already—and this goes back to 1965—to call in its turn for deconstructive questions. Lacan at that time, as has frequently been mentioned here, referred habitually, in a frequent, decisive, self-confident, and sometimes incantatory way, to Heideggerian speech, to the *logos* interpreted by Heidegger, to the truth, which, moreover, was just as often taken in the sense of adequation as it was in the sense of veiling/unveiling. There is no point in recalling here once again that deconstruction, if there is any, is not a critique, still less a theoretical or speculative operation methodically carried out by someone; rather, if there is any deconstruction, it takes place (which I have said too often, and yet once again in *Psyché*, to dare to repeat it again) as experience of the impossible.

I attempted to show this in "Le facteur de la vérité" and elsewhere; I would be unable to reconstitute all this here in so little time.

So here is the form of the chiasmus: I found myself at the time faced with a powerful philosophical, philosophizing reconstitution of psychoanalysis that articulated, assumed, and linked up, with the greatest consistency and consequence, all the motifs that elsewhere were offering themselves, although not without resistance, to something like a genealogico-deconstructive interpretation. At the same time, of course, it was not a matter of regretting, still less of opposing this philosophical restructuration of the psychoanalytic discourse or institutions, this philosophical and thus critical questioning. In also putting to work what is most vital in philosophy, linguistics, anthropology, in displacing and reformalizing them in turn in an original fashion, it was so much more interesting than what was then going about in a dogmatic slumber under the name of psychoanalysis. This chiasmus or, as Major put it, this criss-cross was all the more paradoxical in that there was an impulse coming from psychoanalysis in general—ever since Freud, whom I was trying as well to read in my own, not very Lacanian way, in "Freud and the Scene of Writing"—to deconstruct the privilege of presence, at least as consciousness and egological consciousness. In an apparently external but doubtless not fortuitous fashion, this impulse was converging with the necessity of deconstructing this privilege according to other paths, other questions, those with which I was involved elsewhere (readings of Husserl, Heidegger, the question of writing and literature, and so forth). With the result that the discourse that was at the same time the closest and the most deconstructible, the one that was most to be deconstructed, was no doubt Lacan's. This was already signaled in *Of Grammatology* in 1965–66 with regard to the primacy of the signifier.

That is why, as I said in *Positions* in 1971, four years before publishing "Le facteur de la vérité" (Major mentioned this a moment ago), my theoretical "coming-to-terms" *with* Lacan "consisted in pursuing my own work according to its specific pathways and requirements, whether or not this work should encounter Lacan's, and Lacan's—I do not at all reject the idea—more than any other today."[9]

Was this not a way of saying that I loved and admired him a lot? And of paying homage to him, in a way that pleased me? It is in this same text that I said, with and without philosophy, *with* and *without* Lacan, "truth is necessary" [*il faut la vérité*].

So, since then? Since then, have we exited from this chiasmus? I do not believe we have. Given this chiasmus, which made Lacan's discourse too philosophical for me, too much at home *with the philosophers*—despite, of course, all sorts of disavowals on this subject—too much at home with all those with whom I was in the process, not of breaking, which makes no sense, as I've said countless times, but of reconsidering all the contracts; a Lacanian discourse, then, too much at home with a Sartrian neo-existentialism (which has not been sufficiently discussed or whose remainders have not been sufficiently pointed out in Lacan's discourse right up to *Ecrits*, where the discourse of alienation, authenticity, and so forth prevails), too much at home with Hegel/Kojève the "master" (and Hegel/Kojève is also Heidegger, for Kojève does not anthropologize only the phenomenology of spirit; he also Heideggerianizes it, as you know, which was very interesting—and there would be much to say about this, but I'm obliged to step up the pace here: Elisabeth Roudinesco gave us much to think about the other evening regarding this sequence). Given this chiasmus, which made of Lacan's discourse one that was too much at home with the philosophers and with Heidegger (and from 1965 on, my own reading of Heidegger was anything but "at home" there and explicitly raised questions that I have continued to elaborate constantly *since*), I myself could not be *with* Lacan the way a philosopher would be with a psychoanalyst. If I have lived *with* Lacan, if I have come to terms *with* him at my own rhythm, if I have discussed *with* him, this *being-with* has certainly not been that of a philosopher *with* a psychoanalyst. Anyway, if that had been the case, my place in this odd couple's *ménage* will certainly not have been that of the philosopher, and still less that of someone from the University or the Academy, for which it seemed to me that Lacan always harbored, to my astonishment, an intense or even avid desire. His only excuse, as regards the university, is that he was not part of it. No doubt Lacan would have liked me to play this role of academic philosopher. But to take someone, me, for example, to be an academic philosopher on the pretext that he gets paid for that by an institution, to identify him with or reduce him to that function on this pretext is above all not to read. This impulsive gesture, which is as self-interested as it is defensive, is more or less symmetrical—not altogether but more or less—with the gesture that would consist in taking an analyst for an analyst on the pretext that that is what he or she gets paid for: I have always avoided that gesture.

To say a little more about this chiasmus, all of whose textual and theoretical effects I cannot reconstitute (for that one would need years of minutely detailed and unflinching reading), I will take just one example. From the "Seminar on 'The Purloined Letter' " (thus from *Ecrits*), we'll take, for example, what tightly adjoins and binds a certain number of motifs, which we'll limit arbitrarily to eight in order to suggest the standing institution of the infinite.

1. The motif of the proper and circular trajectory, of the reappropriating trajectory of the letter that returns to the circumscribable place of lack from which it had become detached, that letter about which Lacan says that "since it can be diverted, it must have a course *which is its own* [qui lui est propre]"[10] and a "straight path,"[11] obviously a circular straight path.

2. The motif of truth as adequation or readequation, in the circular return and the proper trajectory, of the origin to the end, of the place of detachment of the signifier to its place of reattachment—or as unveiling in, I quote, that "passion to unveil which has an object: truth,"[12] the analyst remaining "above all the master of truth,"[13] true speech [*la vraie parole*], authentic and authenticated

by the other in sworn faith, being no longer speaking truly [*la parole vraie*][14] and this unveiling being the relay of adequation ("speech appears thus all the more truly speech when its truth is less grounded in what is called adequation to the thing").[15]

3. The motif of "present speech," "full speech" ("I might as well be categorical: in psychoanalytic anamnesis, it is not a question of reality, but of truth, because the effect of full speech is to reorder past contingencies by conferring on them the sense of necessities to come [thus, full speech and future anterior], such as they are constituted by the little freedom through which the subject makes them present");[16] "Analysis can have for its goal only the advent of a true speech [*la parole vraie*] and the realization by the subject of his history in relation to a future."[17]

4. The disqualification (whose spirit is also very Heideggerian in its relation to technics) of the "record," the "recording," and of the mechanical archive as "alienating": "But precisely because it comes to him through an alienated form, even a retransmission of his own recorded discourse, albeit from the mouth of his own doctor, cannot have the same effects as psychoanalytic interlocution"[18]— which therefore must be direct, live, immediate, and so forth. Thus "full speech" that "is defined through its identity with that of which it speaks."[19] This point is very important for me—perhaps I'll return to it—because it links phono-logocentrism or phallogo-centrism to the analytic situation without technical interposition, without an archiving apparatus of repetition, without essential iterability: a very old philosopheme, from Plato up to and including Heidegger.

5. The transcendental position of the phallus, "the privileged signifier of that mark in which the role of the logos is joined to the advent of desire,"[20] a transcendental position that is nothing other than the doctrine that links truth to castration and, I quote, to "the mother's lack of the penis in which the nature of the phallus is revealed."[21]

6. Phonocentrism, which was at the time militant ("A writing, like the dream itself, may be figurative, but like language it is always

articulated symbolically, or even *phonematically* just like language, and in fact phonetically, from the moment it is readable."[22] As I pointed out in "Le facteur de la vérité," this "fact has the value of *fact* only within the ethnocultural limits of so-called phonetic systems of writing, which moreover are never phonetic through and through—otherwise there would not even be a symbolic order. This explicit and massive phonocentrism will be contradicted by Lacan himself, as if it were nothing, as if it had always been so [future anterior of the after-the-fact], in 1972–73, not "before" but after "any grammatology," as I will show in a moment).

7. The misrecognition or the failure to take account of the literary structure of narration, the omission of the frame, of the play of signatures, and notably of its parergonal effect; I cannot reproduce the demonstration I gave in 1975 of this misrecognition, but it is not by chance that the misrecognition, particularly in its treatment of the general narrator, resembles what Nicole Loraux and Philippe Lacoue-Labarthe talked about as a hasty collapse of the choir, the characters, and the spectators in the theater or in tragedy, producing thereby incalculable damage in the reading at the very moment it permits a certain formalizing calculation of psychoanalytic hermeneutics.

8. A spiriting away of the effects of the double in Poe's story, effects which, as I believe I have also shown, ought to have blurred the borders between the imaginary and the symbolic, and thus the strictness of this tripartion to which, as you know, Lacan was also obliged to return much later.

These eight motifs—and no doubt other secondary ones that I don't have time to list—are strongly articulated among themselves; in fact they are indissociable and indispensable to the chief affirmation, which is fundamental, moreover, for both the destiny and the possibility of psychoanalysis, the chief affirmation *with* which it seemed to me urgent and strategically necessary to come to terms, namely, to quote the last words of the seminar: "Thus is it that what the 'purloined letter,' nay, the 'letter in sufferance,' means is that a letter always arrives at its destination."[23] Now this conclusion

was possible only insofar as the letter (which for Lacan is not the
signifier, but the place of the signifier) is not divided. Lacan says
that it "does not suffer partition": "Cut a letter into small pieces,"
he says, "and it remains the letter it is."[24] Consequently, what
Lacan then calls the "materiality of the signifier," which he deduces
from an indivisibility that is nowhere to be found, always seemed
and still seems to me to correspond to an "idealization" of the letter,
to an ideal identity of the letter, which was a problem I had been
working on elsewhere along other lines for quite some time. But—
and I will limit myself to this one point in our context and given
the time at our disposal—I could articulate this question and this
objection (on which, as it could be shown, everything else depends:
another logic of the event and of destination, another thinking of
singularity, the dissemination of the unique beyond a logic of
castration, and so forth), I could read, then, this surreptitious
idealization, not to say this idealism of Lacan's, as Stephen Melville
put it, only on the basis of a work that was already underway, in a
deconstructive mode, with the philosophers, and notably as concerns the constitution of idealities, of ideal objects in Husserl.
Without pursuing this any further, suffice it to say that in order to
read Lacan, to read him in a problematizing and nondogmatic
fashion, it is also necessary to read, for example, Husserl and a few
others, and to read them in a problematic or deconstructive way.
There is here, if I may be permitted to say so, the outline of a new
training, another curriculum for psychoanalyst readers of Lacan, at
least if they want to read him otherwise than in an apelike, ortho-
dox, and defensive manner. This parallels, in sum, the advice
concerning a "new training" that certain of us—the rare professional philosophers who read and published on Lacan in the
philosophical university (I am thinking above all of Philippe
Lacoue-Labarthe and Jean-Luc Nancy)—gave to philosophers
when we told them to read Lacan, which advice was then, about
twenty years ago, rather rare. (If I had the time, I would explain
why in my opinion all the texts of the "professional philosophers"
to whom I have just referred are not read and are not readable in
France, particularly by most French "Lacanians.")

3. Second Protocol: The Future Anterior
    of the After-the-Fact

I have said that my reading of the "Seminar on 'The Purloined
Letter'" as well as what prefigured it from 1965 to 1971 in *Of
Grammatology* and *Positions* did not claim to enclose or exhaust
Lacan (I said so explicitly in these very texts), but only to treat a
strong and relatively stabilized configuration of Lacanian displacement. The discourse of Lacan, which was always very sensitive to
any movement on the theoretical scene—and who could blame
him?—continued thereafter to readjust, even recast, sometimes
contradict the axioms I have just mentioned. After 1968, the accent
put on writing continued to become more pronounced, to the
point of inverting, very "grammatologically," the utterance I cited a
moment ago concerning "phonematic and even always phonetic"
writing, since he could write in the seminar *Encore*: "But the
signifier can in no way be limited to this phonematic support."[25]
Earlier, René Major cited certain spectacular examples—there are
many more beginning at this time—of this sudden substitution of
the graphematic for the phonematic (which, moreover, interests
me here only as a symptomatic index in the history of ideas, as we
used to say, and not in itself, since what I proposed calling trace,
gramme, differance, and so forth is no more graphic than it is
phonematic, no more spatial than temporal; but let's drop the
subject, since this is not the place to take up this serious and
tenacious misunderstanding). This kind of substitution of writing
for speech around 1970 deserves its own history and is not limited
to Lacan. Ponge told me one day, with a smile, that he was
rereading his texts to see whether he had not given in too much to
phonocentrism and whether he could replace speech by writing
here and there without too much damage. Roger Laporte drew up a
list, which I found to be as illuminating as it was remorseless, of all
the places where, during the same years, our friend Maurice
Blanchot, when he republished his old texts in collections, had
simply replaced "speech" by "writing." I am not sure that it is a

matter of a *Kehre*, as Stephen Melville put it, but if one were to open the question of the *Kehre*, then it would be very general.

All of this merely to say that the historical narration of what remained and still remains—above all for me—the future of Lacanian thought as it moves beyond *Ecrits* is all the more difficult in that Lacan was an incomparable listener and his discursive machine was one of such sensitivity that everything could be inscribed there with finesse or discretion. (This is quite all right; who doesn't try to do the same?) But, what is more, it is inscribed there in the spoken words of a seminar that, by giving rise to numerous stenotyped or tape-recorded archivings, will have then fallen prey not only to all the problems of rights (which I don't want to get into here and which M. Conté will have evoked in passing the other day), but also to all the problems posed by the delays of publishing and of an editing—in the American sense—that was of the most active sort. Since all of these things hang by a hair, since the stakes get decided in a word, an ellipsis, a verbal modality, a conditional or a future anterior, especially when one knows Lacan's rhetoric, I say good luck to any narrator who would try to know what was said and written by whom on which date: what would Lacan have said or not have said! This is also at bottom the problem of the letter and destination that separates me perhaps most closely from [*d'avec*] Lacan.

4. Third Protocol: Chiasmatic Invagination
   of the Borders

Not only were my references to Lacan, and in particular to the "Seminar on 'The Purloined Letter,' " not totalizing, homogenizing, or critical, but I even conceded he was right as concerns reason, the question of reason remaining open, as well as the question of what happens when one concedes to another, that is, when one gives reason or, as we say in French, *donne raison*. In *The Post Card*, I said that he was right about "the reason for a characteristic [*trait*] that had never before been elucidated, and which shows once again the depth of Freud's intuition: namely, why he advances the view that there is only one *libido*, his text showing that he conceives it as masculine in nature."[26] Saying Lacan is right (just as the signatory of "Envois" begins by saying the beloved other is right: "Yes, you were right"), "Le facteur de la vérité" speaks, as concerns precisely this "characteristic [*trait*] that had never before been elucidated," of a trait drawn from reason or a check [*traite*] drawn on reason. "In the logic said to be 'of the kettle' (a check drawn on reason), reason will always be right" (482–83). Saying Lacan is right or doing right by Lacan [*raison donnée . . . ou rendue*] makes my text still more unreadable for readers in a rush to decide between the "pro and the con," in short, for those minds who believed I was opposing Lacan or showing him to be wrong. The question lies elsewhere: it is the question of reason and of the principle of reason. Thus, not only was I not criticizing Lacan, but I was not even writing a sort of overseeing or objectifying metadiscourse *on* Lacan or *on* a text of Lacan's. My writing involved me in a scene, which scene I was showing at the same time (no doubt in small phrases that no one reads) could not be closed or framed. All of this has *since* been constantly put back into play in other scenes *en abyme* that have been deployed here and there, more often there than here, which is to say, once again, abroad. Moreover, for all these reasons, the argument of "Le facteur de la vérité" does not lend itself to being framed in the text bearing this title; it is played, set adrift in *The Post Card*, the book with that title, which inscribes "Le facteur de la vérité" like a piece in a borderless fiction, neither public nor private, *with* and *without* a general narrator. It is inscribed first of all in "Envois," of which I am not the signatory and where a little-read plot involving a wandering letter, some remarks on destination as well as on the analytic institution and what then happens, or not, demonstrate, while doing it, that which is uttered there without lending itself to some meta-utterance. I will take only one example, if I may be permitted to quote a character from this book without quoting myself (that is my excuse), from "Envois" dated August 18, 1979:

18 August 1979. Is it true that you call me only when I'm not there?
One day you told me
that I was a torch   "come"
which is not valid without the tone, without the timbre, without the
voice of mine that you know. So much for the fire.

They had put everything on a picture (of the
one, of the other, of the couple), and then they remained attached to
the betting, and they are still speculating but they are no longer there.
Each of them to the other: you were in league to destroy me, you
conspired, you have covered all the trails, get out of it yourself.

And this short philosophical dia-
logue for your amusement. "—What is it, a destination?—There where
it arrives.—So then everywhere that it arrives there was destination?—
Yes.—But not before?—No.—That's convenient, since if it arrives
there, it is that it was destined to arrive there. But then one can only
say so after the fact?—When it has arrived, it is indeed the proof that it
had to arrive, and arrive there, at its destination.—But before arriving,
it is not destined, for example it neither desires nor demands any
address? There is everything that arrives where it had to arrive, but no
destination before the arrival?—Yes, but I meant to say something
else.—Of course, that's what I was saying.—There you are."

As I gave her to understand, I don't
know if she was right to write *what* she wrote, and this is quite
secondary, but in any event she was right to write it. Right *a priori*. I
know nothing about how it happens, how it arrives for her, and it
won't be soon either, it's only just beginning, but she cannot have been
wrong to send herself that (244–45).

This "envoi" relayed two other postscripts, one within the other
(which you will pardon me for reading as well, but you may
presume that they are not by me). They situated, I believe, one of
the essential places in the ongoing and interminable discussion
with Lacan, namely, the thinking of contingency, singularity, the
event, the encounter, chance, and *tukhē*, which is also a certain
thinking, interpretation, or experience of death whose signifier
would be the phallus; all of which could summarize the unanswered questions I am still today putting to Lacan, *with* whom it is
worth discussing: questions on the subject of what he has to say on,

in effect, being, man, animals (especially animals), and thus God—
no less.

P.S. I forgot, you are completely right: one of the paradoxes of destination, is that if you wanted *to demonstrate*, for someone, that something
never arrives at its destination, it's all over. The demonstration, once it
had reached its end, would have proved what it was not supposed to
demonstrate. But this is why, dear friend, I always say "a letter *can*
always *not* arrive at its destination, etc." This is a chance.*
                                        You know that I never say that
I'm right and never demonstrate anything. They put up with this very
badly, consequently they would like nothing to have happened, everything wiped off the map. Wait for me.

*P.S. Finally a chance, if you will, if you yourself can, and if you have it,
the chance (*tukhē*, fortune, this is what I mean, good fortune, good
fate: us). The mischance (the mis-address) of this chance is that in
order *to be able* not to arrive, it must bear within itself a force and a
structure, a straying of the destination, such that it *must* also not arrive
in any way. Even in arriving (always to some "subject"), the letter takes
itself away *from the arrival at arrival.* It arrives elsewhere, always several
times. You can no longer take hold of it. It is the structure of the letter
(as post card, in other words, the fatal partition that it must support)
which demands this, I have said it elsewhere, delivered to a *facteur*
subject to the same law. The letter demands this, right here, and you
too, you demand it. (123–24)

This thinking of the destination is indissociable, of course, from
a thinking of death, from destination as death—and that is why I
allowed myself to recall this barely private thing, between Lacan
and me: the fact that, at each of our encounters, it was a question of
death and that it was Lacan alone who spoke of it.
   What binds destination to death is said by the signatory of
"Envois," for example:

Murder is everywhere, my unique and immense one. We are the worst
criminals in history. And right here I kill you, save, save, you, save you
run away, the unique, the living one over there whom I love. Understand me, when I write, right here, on these innumerable post cards, I

annihilate not only what I am saying but also the unique addressee that I constitute, and therefore every possible addressee, and every destination. I kill you, I annul you at my fingertips, wrapped around my finger. To do so it suffices only that I be legible—and I become illegible to you, you are dead. If I say that I write for dead addressees, not dead in the future but already dead at the moment when I get to the end of a sentence, it is not in order to play. Genet said that his theater was addressed to the dead and I take it like that on the train in which I am going writing you without end. The addressees are dead, the destination is death: no, not in the sense of S. or p.'s predication, according to which we would be destined to die, no, not in the sense in which to arrive at our destination, for us mortals, is to end by dying. (33)

Well, pardon me for these readings, which lead me to hasten my conclusion with three remarks that I will make as brief and elliptical as possible:

1. death;
2. the analytic situation;
3. the "is there a psychoanalysis?" in general or some properly namable psychoanalysis, namable by a proper name?

1. On death: *since*, since all the texts I have just mentioned, I feel increasingly tempted not to accept the discourse on being-for-death, in either its Heideggerian form or the Lacanian form in which it is linked to the phallocentered signifier, without a lot of questions in return, questions of all sorts, and without a lot of displacements that are also experiences and not only speculative discourses, discussions, or even critical objections. But I can't say more about this here; these things are happening elsewhere, in recent seminars, in relation to the questions of the animal and of God. (The remarkable things Lacan says on the animal are also in my view most problematic. In short, it would be a matter of contesting that death happens to some mortal being-for-death; rather, and this is a scandal for sense and for good sense, it happens only to some immortal who lacks for lacking nothing. I am thinking here of a certain passage in *Zarathustra* on the suffering that

arises from a lack of lack and that, in the course of my seminar this year on "Eating the Other," I interpreted in a direction that perhaps intersects with what Nancy was saying the other evening.) In "Le facteur de la vérité," at the conclusion of an analysis of "the lack that is never lacking (in its place)," I pointed out the following, which at the time seemed to me to situate very well the difference "with" Lacan: "The difference which interests me here is that—a formula to be understood as one will—the lack does not have its place in dissemination" (441).

2. On the analytic situation: another recollection from my meeting with Lacan. In this case, I was not a direct witness—and the question of the archive is thus posed in yet a different manner. René Girard reported to me that after my lecture in Baltimore, when he was seeking to elicit from Lacan his own (generous) assessment, Lacan supposedly replied: "Yes, yes, it's good, but the difference between him and me is that he does not deal with people who are suffering," meaning by that: people in analysis. What did he know about that? Very careless. To be able to say such a thing, so imperturbably, and know such a thing, he could not have been referring either to suffering (alas, I too deal with people who suffer—all of you, for example) or to transference, that is, to love, which has never needed the analytic situation to claim its victims. Lacan thus made clinical treatment, institutionalized in a certain mode, and the rules governing the analytic situation into criteria of absolute competence for speaking—about all this. Here is a better-known episode that occurred some ten years later after Lacan had used the future anterior several times to reappropriate by way of antedating (when he said, for example, that he was giving up certain concepts and words[27]—for instance, gramme and other similar things, of which as far as I know he never made any use and which, instead of giving up, he should have simply taken up). In a session of the seminar in 1977 (still "l'Insu-que-sait"), Lacan made a compulsive blunder: he said that he thought I was in analysis (laughter from the audience, the sentence replaced by an ellipsis in *Ornicar*, but too late because the transcription had circulated; once

again the problem of the archive, the archive that no one can master, here no more than ever because of this recording technique). The thing has now been recounted and commented on in *The Post Card* (202–4). Elisabeth Roudinesco cites it but only in the official version from *Ornicar*, with its ellipsis. Meanwhile, since the legal archive covers less and less of the whole archive, this archive remains unmasterable and continues on its way, in continuity with the anarchive.

In any case, what did he know about it, whether or not I was in analysis, and what could that mean? The fact that I have never been in analysis, in the institutional sense of the analytic situation, does not mean that I am not, here or there, in a way that cannot be easily toted up, analysand and analyst in my own time and in my own way. Like everyone else. In a remark that has been archived by the recording machines but forever withdrawn from the official archive, Lacan says this (notice and admire the syntax and the reference to nonknowledge and truth): "someone about whom I did not know that—to tell the truth I believe he is in analysis— about whom I did not know that he was in analysis—but this is merely a hypothesis—his name is Jacques Derrida, who has written a preface to this *Verbier*."[28] This nonknowledge in truth of a belief ("to tell the truth I believe he is in analysis"!), of a simple hypothesis, concerned therefore the being-in-analysis of someone whom he, Lacan, was not afraid to name, the being-in-analysis with a couple of analysts ("for he couples them," added Lacan, who was then obviously unaware of the fact that one of the two, who was my friend, was dead by the time I wrote the preface in question, which was thus written to his memory, as homage, and in his absence).

How could Lacan make his listeners laugh on the subject or on the basis of a blunder, his own, concerning a hypothetical analysand—even as he himself presented himself (and this is, moreover, one of his most interesting assertions) as an analysand, a master of truth as analysand and not as analyst? How could he insist on two occasions on my real status as institutional nonanalyst and on what he wrongly supposed to be my status as institutional analysand, whereas he ought to have been the first to cast suspicion on the limits or borders of these sites, to pay attention to the tangled knots of this invagination?

3. This leads to my last point. However insufficient, intermittent, distracted, or floating my interminable listening to Lacan may be, what keeps it on alert is less the question of philosophy, science, or psychoanalysis than another question, which concerns a certain dominant state (meaning the dominance of the master) of the history of philosophy, science, psychoanalysis, namely, the dominant state that at a certain point I called phallogocentrism, according to a certain historical, precarious, conventional, and finite determination of the analytic situation, of its rules and its limits. To this analytic situation, it seems to me, one might aptly apply the topological expression that I ventured in another circumstance: the chiasmatic invagination of the borders. I proposed the expression in "Pas" in *Parages*, which I thank Stephen Melville for having mentioned here.

If this is indeed how things are, the question of knowing *whether or not there is* some psychoanalysis—X-ian, his, yours, mine—that can hold up or that is coming, this incalculable, unimaginable, unaccountable, unattributable question is displaced to the degree that the analytic situation, and thus the analytic institution, is deconstructed, *as if by itself*, without deconstruction or deconstructive project. As for the relations between this deconstruction as experience of the impossible and the "there is," I have spoken of them elsewhere; it is archived.

What will I not have said today! But if I had said that we loved each other very much, Lacan and I, and thus we promised each other very much, and that this was for me a good thing in this life, would I have been in the truth? Stephen Melville said that the promise always risked being also a threat.

That's true. But I would always prefer to prefer the promise.

§ 3 "To Do Justice to Freud":
The History of Madness in
the Age of Psychoanalysis

To the memory of Georges Canguilhem

When Elisabeth Roudinesco and René Major did me the honor and kindness of inviting me to a commemoration that would also be a reflection, to one of these genuine tributes where thought is conditioned by fidelity and fidelity honed by thought, I did not hesitate for one moment.

Above all, because I love memory. This is nothing original, of course, and yet, how else can one love? Indeed, thirty years ago this great book of Foucault was an event whose repercussions were so intense and multiple that I will not even try to identify, much less measure, them deep inside me. Next, because I love friendship, and the trusting affection that Foucault showed me thirty years ago, which was to last for many years, was all the more precious in that, being shared, it corresponded to my professed admiration for him. Then, after 1972, what came to obscure this friendship, without, however, affecting my admiration, was not in fact alien to this book, and to a certain debate that ensued—or at least to its distant, delayed, and indirect effects. There was in all of this a sort of dramatic chain of events, a compulsive and repeated precipitation that I do not wish to describe here because I do not wish to be alone, to be the only one to speak of this after the death of Michel Foucault—except to say that this shadow that made us invisible to one another, that made us not associate with one another for close to ten years (until January 1, 1982, when I returned from a Czech prison), is still part of a story that I love like life itself. It is part of a story or history that is related, and that by the same token relates me, to the book we are commemorating here, to something like its postface, one of its postfaces, since the drama I just alluded to arose out of a certain postface, even out of a sort of postscript added by Foucault to a postface in 1972.

While accepting wholeheartedly this generous invitation, I nonetheless declined the accompanying suggestion that I return to the discussion that began some twenty-eight years ago. I declined for numerous reasons, the first being the one I just mentioned: one does not carry on a stormy discussion after the other has departed. Second, because this whole thing is more than overdetermined (so many difficult and intersecting texts—Descartes's, Foucault's—so many objections and responses, from me but also from all those, in France and elsewhere, who later came to act as arbiters); it has become too distant from me, and perhaps because of the drama just alluded to I no longer wished to return to it. In the end, the debate is archived and those who might be interested can analyze it as much as they want and decide for themselves. By rereading all the texts of this discussion, right up to the last word, and especially the last word, one will better be able to understand, I imagine, why I prefer not to give it a new impetus today. There is no privileged witness for such a situation—which, moreover, can only ever take form with the possible disappearance of the witness already at the origin. This is perhaps one of the meanings of any history of madness, one of the problems for any project or discourse concerning a history of madness, or even a history of sexuality: Is there any witnessing to madness? Who can witness? Does witnessing mean seeing? Is it to provide a reason [*rendre raison*]? Does it have an object? Is there any object? Is there a possible third that might provide a reason without objectifying, or even identifying, that is to say, without examining [*arraisoner*]?

Though I have decided not to return to what was debated close to thirty years ago, it would nevertheless be absurd, obsessional to the point of pathological, to say nothing of impossible, to give in to a sort of fetishistic denial and to think that I can protect myself from any contact with the place or meaning of this discussion. Although I intend to speak today of something else altogether, starting from a very recent rereading of *The History of Madness in the Classical Age,* I am not surprised, and you will probably not be either, to see the silhouette of certain questions reemerge: not their content, of course, to which I will in no way return, but their abstract type, the schema or specter of an analogous problematic. If I speak not of Descartes but of Freud, for example, if I thus avoid a figure who seems central to this book and who, because he is decisive as regards its center or centering of perspective, emerges right from the early pages on, right from the first border or approach,[1] if I thus avoid this Cartesian reference in order to move toward another (psychoanalysis, Freudian or some other) that is evoked only on the edges of the book and is named only right near the end, or ends, on the other border, this will perhaps be once again in order to pose a question that will resemble the one that imposed itself upon me thirty years ago, namely, that of the very possibility of a history of madness. The question will be, in the end, about the same, though it will be posed from another border, and it still imposes itself upon me as the first tribute owed such a book. If this book was possible, if it had from the beginning and retains today a certain monumental value, the presence and undeniable necessity of a *monument,* that is, of what imposes itself by recalling and cautioning, it must tell us, teach us, or ask us something about its own possibility.

About its own possibility *today*: yes, we are saying *today,* a certain today. Whatever else one may think of this book, whatever questions or reservations it might inspire in those who come at it from some other point of view, its pathbreaking force seems incontestable. Just as incontestable as the law according to which all pathbreaking opens the way only at a certain price, only, that is, by bolting shut other passages, by ligaturing, stitching up, or compressing, indeed repressing, at least provisionally, other veins. And so today, like yesterday, I mean in March of 1963, this question of the *today* is important to me, the question I tried to formulate yesterday. I ask you to pardon me this once, then, since I will not make a habit of it, for citing a few lines that then defined, in its general form, a task that seems to me still necessary, on the side of [*du côté de*] Freud this time rather than on the side of Descartes. By saying "on the side of Freud" rather than "on the side of Descartes," let us not give in too quickly to the naiveté that would precipitate us into believing that we are closer to a today with Freud than with Descartes, though this is the opinion of most historians.

Here, then, is the question of yesterday, of the today of yesterday, as I would translate it today, on the side of Freud, transporting it in this way into the today of today:

> Therefore, if Foucault's book, despite all the acknowledged impossibilities and difficulties [acknowledged by him, of course], was capable of being written, we have the right to ask what, in the last resort, supports this language without recourse or support ["without recourse" and "without support" are expressions of Foucault that I had just cited]: who enunciates the possibility of nonrecourse? Who wrote and who is to understand, in what language and from what historical situation of logos, who wrote and who is to understand this history of madness? For it is not by chance that such a project could take shape today. Without forgetting, *quite to the contrary*, the audacity of Foucault's act in the *History of Madness*, we must assume that a certain liberation of madness has gotten underway, that psychiatry has opened itself up, however minimally [and, in the end, I would be tempted simply to replace *psychiatry* by *psychoanalysis* in order to translate the today of yesterday into the today of my question of today], and that the concept of madness as unreason, if it ever had a unity, has been dislocated. And that a project such as Foucault's can find its historical origin and passageway in the opening produced by this dislocation.
>
> If Foucault, more than anyone else, is attentive and sensitive to these kinds of questions, it nevertheless appears that he does not acknowledge their quality of being prerequisite methodological or philosophical considerations.[2]

If this type of question made any sense or had any legitimacy, if the point was then to question that which, today, in this time that is ours, this time in which Foucault's *History of Madness* was written, made possible the event of such a discourse, it would have been more appropriate for me to elaborate this problematic on the side of modernity, *a parte subjecti*, in some sense, on the side where the book was written, thus on the side, for example, of what must have happened to the modern psychiatry mentioned in the passage I just read. To modern psychiatry or, indeed, to psychoanalysis, or rather to psychoanalyses or psychoanalysts, since the passage to the plural will be precisely what is at stake in this discussion. It would have thus been more imperative to insist on modern psychiatry or psychoanalysis than to direct the same question toward Descartes. To study the place and role of psychoanalysis in the Foucauldian project of a history of madness, as I am now going to try to do, might thus consist in correcting an oversight or in confronting more directly a problematic that I had left in a preliminary stage, as a general, programmatic frame, in the introduction to my lecture of 1963. That lecture made only one allusion to psychoanalysis. It is true, however, that it inscribed it from the very opening. In a protocol that laid out certain reading positions, I spoke of the way in which philosophical language is rooted in nonphilosophical language, and I recalled a rule of hermeneutical method that still seems to me valid for the historian of philosophy as well as for the psychoanalyst, namely, the necessity of first ascertaining a surface or manifest meaning and, thus, of speaking the language of the patient to whom one is listening: the necessity of gaining a good understanding, in a quasi-scholastic way, philologically and grammatically, by taking into account the dominant and stable conventions, of what Descartes *meant* on the already so difficult surface of his text, such as it is interpretable according to classical norms of reading; the necessity of gaining this understanding *before* submitting the first reading to a symptomatic and historical interpretation regulated by other axioms or protocols, *before and in order to* destabilize, wherever this is possible and if it is necessary, the authority of canonical interpretations. Whatever one ends up doing with it, one must begin by listening to the canon. It is in this context that I recalled Ferenczi's remark cited by Freud in *The Interpretation of Dreams* ("Every language has its own dream language") and Lagache's observations concerning polyglotism in analysis.[3]

In its general and historical form, my question concerned the *site* that *today* gives rise to a history of madness and thereby makes it possible. Such a question should have led me, it is true, toward the situation of psychiatry and psychoanalysis rather than toward a questioning of a reading of Descartes. This logic would have seemed more natural, and the consequence more immediate. But if, in so strictly delimiting the field, I substituted Descartes for Freud, it was perhaps not only because of the significant and strategic place that Foucault confers upon the Cartesian moment in the interpretation of the *Great Confinement* and of the *Classical Age*, that is to say, in the layout of the very object of the book; it was already, at least implicitly, because of the role that the reference to a certain Descartes played in the thought of that time, in the early sixties, as close as possible to psychoanalysis, in the very element, in truth, of a certain psychoanalysis and Lacanian theory. This theory developed around the question of the subject and the subject of science. Whether it was a question of anticipated certainty and logical time (1945, in *Ecrits*) or, some years later (1965–66), of the role of the cogito and—precisely—of the deceitful God in "La Science et la vérité," Lacan returned time and again to a certain unsurpassability of Descartes.[4] In 1945, Lacan associated Descartes with Freud in his "Propos sur la causalité psychique" and concluded by saying that "neither Socrates, nor Descartes, nor Marx, nor Freud, can be 'surpassed' insofar as they led their research with this passion for unveiling whose object is the truth."[5]

The title I have proposed for the few reflections I will risk today, "The History of Madness in the Age of Psychoanalysis," clearly indicates a change—a change in tense, in mode, or in voice. It is no longer a question of the age *described* by a *History of Madness*. It is no longer a question of an epoch or period, such as the classical age, that would, inasmuch as it is its very object, stand before the history of madness as Foucault writes it. It is a question today of the age to which the book itself belongs, the age out of which it takes place, the age that provides its situation; it is a question of the age that is *describing* rather than the age that is *described*. In my title, "the history of madness" must be in quotation marks since the title designates the age of the book, *The History (historia rerum ges-tarum) of Madness*—as a book—in the age of psychoanalysis and not the history (*res gestae*) of madness, of madness itself, in the age of psychoanalysis, even though, as we will see, Foucault regularly attempts to objectify psychoanalysis and to reduce it to that of which he speaks rather than to that out of which he speaks. What will interest me will thus be the time and historical conditions in which the book is rooted, those that it takes as its point of depar-ture, and not so much the time or historical conditions that it recounts and tries in a certain sense to objectify. Were one to trust too readily in the opposition between subject and object, as well as in the category of objectification (something that I here believe to be neither possible nor just, and hardly faithful to Foucault's own intention), one would say for the sake of convenience that it is a question of considering the history of madness *a parte subjecti*, that is, from the side where it is written or inscribed and not from the side of what it describes.

Now, from the side where this history is written, there is, of course, a certain state of psychiatry—as well as psychoanalysis. Would Foucault's project have been possible without psycho-analysis, with which it is contemporary and of which it speaks little and in such an equivocal or ambivalent manner in the book? Does the project owe psychoanalysis anything? What? Would the debt, if it had been contracted, be essential? Or would it, on the contrary, define the very thing from which the project had to detach itself, in a critical fashion, in order to take shape? In a word, what is the situation of psychoanalysis at the moment of, and with respect to, Foucault's book? And how does this book situate its project with respect not only to psychoanalysis in general, but to a particular psychoanalysis, at a particular phase of its history, in one or another of its figures?

Let us put our trust for a moment in this common name, psychoanalysis. And let us delay a bit the arrival of proper names, for example, Freud or Lacan, and provisionally assume that there is indeed a psychoanalysis that is a single whole: as if it were not, already in Freud, sufficiently divided to make its localization and identification more than problematic. Yet the very thing whose coming due we are here trying to delay will no doubt form the very horizon, in any case the provisional conclusion, of this talk.

Foucault speaks little of Freud in this book. This may seem justified, on the whole, by the delimitation that a historian of madness in the classical age must impose upon himself. If one accepts the great caesura of this layout (even though this raises a swarm of questions, which I prudently, and by economy, avoid in order to get a better grasp on what Foucault *means* by Freud, situating myself, therefore, within the thesis or hypothesis of the partition between a classical and a postclassical age), then Freud does not have to be treated. He can and must be located, at most, on the borderline. The borderline is never a secure place, it never forms an indivisible line, and it is always on the border that the most disconcerting problems of topology get posed. Where, in fact, would a problem of topology get posed if not *on the border*? Would one ever have to worry about the border if it formed an indivisible line? A borderline is, moreover, not a place per se. It is always risky, particularly for the historian, to assign to whatever happens on the borderline, to whatever happens between sites, the taking place of a determinable event.

Now, Foucault *does and does not want* to situate Freud in a historical place that is stabilizable, identifiable, and open to a univocal understanding. The interpretation or topography of the Freudian moment with which he presents us is always uncertain, divided, mobile, some would say ambiguous, others ambivalent, confused, or contradictory. Sometimes he wants to credit Freud, sometimes discredit him, unless he is actually doing both indiscernibly and at the same time. One will always have the choice of attributing this ambivalence to either Foucault or Freud; it can characterize a motivation, the gesture of the interpreter and a certain state of his work, but it can also, or in the first place, refer simply to the interpreter or historian's taking account of a structural duplicity that his work reflects from the thing itself, namely, from the event of psychoanalysis. The motivation would thus be *justly* motivated, it would be *just that*—motivated; it would be called for and justified by the very thing that is in question. For the ambiguity of which we are going to speak could indeed be on the side of psychoanalysis, on the side of the event of this invention named psychoanalysis.

1. The Hinge—Today

To begin, let us indicate a few telling signs. If most of the explicit references to Freud are grouped in the conclusions of the book (at the end of "The Birth of the Asylum" and in the beginning of "The Anthropological Circle"),[6] what I would here call a *charnière*, a *hinge*, comes earlier on, right in the middle of the volume, to divide at once the book and the book's relation to Freud.

Why a *charnière*? This word can be taken in the technical or anatomical sense of a central or cardinal articulation, a hinge pin (*cardo*) or pivot. A *charnière* or hinge is an axial device that enables the circuit, the trope, or the movement of rotation. But one might also dream a bit in the vicinity of its homonym, that is, in line with this other *artifact* that the code of falconry also calls a *charnière*, the place where the hunter attracts the bird by laying out flesh as a lure.

This double articulation, this double movement or alternation between opening and closing that is assured by the workings of a hinge, this coming and going, indeed this *fort/da* of a pendulum [*pendule*] or balance [*balancier*]—that is what Freud means to Foucault. And this technico-historical hinge also remains the place of a possible simulacrum or lure—for both the body and the flesh.

Taken at this level of generality, things will never change for Foucault. There will always be this interminable, alternating movement that successively opens and closes, draws near and distances, rejects and accepts, excludes and includes, disqualifies and legitimates, masters and liberates. The Freudian place is not only the technico-historical apparatus, the *artifact* called *charnière* or hinge. Freud himself will in fact take on the ambiguous figure of a doorman or doorkeeper [*huissier*]. Ushering in a new epoch of madness, our epoch, the one out of which is written *The History of Madness* (the book bearing this title), Freud also represents the best guardian of an epoch that comes to a close with him, the history of madness such as it is recounted by the book bearing this title.

Freud as the doorman of the today, the holder of the keys, of those that open as well as those that close the door, that is, the *huis*: onto the today [*l'aujourd'hui*] or onto madness. He [*lui*], Freud, is the double figure of the door or the doorkeeper. He stands guard and ushers in. Alternatively or simultaneously, he closes one epoch and opens another. And as we will see, this double possibility is not alien to an institution, to what is called the analytic situation as a scene behind closed doors [*huis clos*]. That is why—and this would be the paradox of a serial law—Freud does and does not belong to the different series in which Foucault inscribes him. What is outstanding, outside the series [*hors-série*], turns out to be regularly reinscribed within different series. I am not now going to get involved in formal questions concerning a quasi-transcendental law of seriality that could be illustrated in an analogous way by so many other examples, each time, in fact, that the transcendental condition of a series is also, paradoxically, a part of that series, creating aporias for the constitution of any set or whole [*ensemble*], particularly, of any historical configuration (age, *episteme*, paradigm, *themata*, epoch, and so on). These aporias are anything but accidental impasses that one should try to force at all costs into received theoretical models. The putting to the test of these aporias is also the chance of thinking.

To keep to the contract of this conference, I will restrict myself to a single example.

The first sign comes right in the middle of the book (*M*, pp. 197–98; *F*, pp. 410–11). It comes at the end of the second part, in the chapter entitled "Doctors and Patients." We have there a sort of epilogue, less than a page and a half long. Separated from the conclusion by asterisks,[7] the epilogue also signals the truth of a transition and the meaning of a passage. It seems to be firmly structured by two unequivocal statements:

1. Psychology does not exist in the classical age. It does *not yet* exist. Foucault says this without hesitation right at the beginning of

the epilogue: "In the classical age, it is futile to try to distinguish physical therapeutics from psychological medications, for the simple reason that psychology did not exist."

2. But as for the psychology that was to be born after the classical age, psychoanalysis would not be a part, it would *no longer* be a part. Foucault writes: "It is not psychology that is involved in psychoanalysis."

In other words, if in the classical age there is *not yet* psychology, there is, in psychoanalysis, *already no more* psychology. But in order to affirm this, it is necessary, *on the one hand*, to resist a prejudice or a temptation, to resist that which continues to urge so many interpreters of good sense (and sometimes, in part, Foucault among them) to take psychoanalysis for a psychology (however original or new it may be). Foucault is going to show signs of this resistance, as we will see. But it is also necessary, *on the other hand*, to accept, within this historical schema, the hypothesis of a return: not the *return to Freud* but the *return of Freud* to—.

What return? Return to what? *Return* is Foucault's word, an underscored word. If psychoanalysis is already *no longer* a psychology, does it not, at least in this respect, seem to suggest a certain return to the time when psychology was *not yet*? Beyond eighteenth-century psychology and, very broadly, beyond the psychologistic modernity of the nineteenth century, beyond the positivist institution of psychology, does it not seem as if Freud were joining back up with a certain classical age or at least with whatever in this age does not determine madness as a psychical illness but as unreason, that is, as something that has to do with reason? In the classical age, if such a thing exists (a hypothesis of Foucault that I take here, in this context, as such, as if it were not debatable), unreason is no doubt reduced to silence; one does not speak with it. One interrupts or forbids dialogue, and this suspension or interdiction would have received from the Cartesian cogito the violent form of a sentence. For Freud *too* madness would be unreason (and in this sense, at least, there would be a neo-Cartesian logic at work in psychoanalysis). But this time one should resume speaking with it: one would reestablish a dialogue with unreason and lift the Cartesian interdiction. Like the word *return*, the expression "dialogue with unreason" is a quotation. The two expressions scan a final paragraph of this epilogue, in the middle of the book, that begins with the phrase with which I entitled this talk: "We must do justice to Freud" (*M*, p. 198; *F*, p. 411).

When one says "one must do justice," "one has to be fair" [*"il faut être juste"*], it is often with the intention of correcting an impulse or reversing the direction of a tendency; one is also recommending resisting a temptation. Foucault must have felt this temptation, the temptation to do an injustice to Freud, to be unfair to him—that is, in this case, to write him into the age of the psychopathological institution (which we will define in a moment). He must have felt it outside or within himself. Indeed, such a temptation must still be threatening and liable to reemerge, since it is still necessary to call for vigilance and greater justice.

Here, then, is the paragraph, which I read in extenso, since its internal tension determines, it seems to me, the matrix of all future statements about psychoanalysis; it determines them in the very oscillation of their movement back and forth. It is like the scales of a justice [*la balance d'une justice*] that not even the death sentence [*arrêt de mort*] could stop [*arrêterait*] in an even or just [*juste*] stability. It is as if justice were to remain its own movement:

> This is why we must do justice to Freud. Between Freud's *Five Case Histories* and Janet's scrupulous investigations of *Psychological Healing*, there is more than the density of a *discovery*; there is the sovereign violence of a *return*. Janet enumerated the elements of a division, drew up his inventory, annexed here and there, perhaps conquered. Freud went back to madness at the level of its *language*, reconstituted one of the essential elements of an experience reduced to silence by positivism; he did not make a major addition to the list of psychological treatments for madness; he restored, in medical thought, the possibility of a dialogue with unreason. Let us not be surprised that the most "psychological" of medications has so quickly encountered its converse and its organic confirmations. It is not psychology that is involved in psychoanalysis: but precisely an experience of unreason

that it has been psychology's meaning, in the modern world, to mask. (*M*, p. 198; *F*, p. 411)[8]

"To mask": positivist psychology would thus have masked the experience of unreason: an imposition of the mask, a violent dissimulation of the face, of truth or of visibility. Such violence would have consisted in disrupting a certain unity, which corresponded precisely [*justement*] to the presumed unity of the classical age: from then on, there would be, on the one hand, illness of an organic nature and, on the other, unreason, an unreason often tempered by this modernity under its "epithetic" form: the *unreasonable*, whose discursive manifestations will become the object of a psychology.[9] This psychology then loses all relation to a certain truth of madness, that is, to a certain truth of Unreason. Psychoanalysis, on the contrary, breaks with psychology *by speaking with the Unreason* that speaks within madness and, thus, by returning through this exchange of words, not to the classical age itself—which also determined madness as Unreason, but, unlike psychology, did so only in order to exclude or confine it—but toward this eve of the classical age, which still haunted it.

While this schema is firmly established by the page just cited, I was struck in rereading *The History of Madness* by a paradox in the form of a chiasmus. I had not, in my first reading, given it the attention it deserves. What is the schema of this chiasmus? By reason of what we have just heard, in order to do "justice" to Freud we ought to give him credit for figuring—as he does occasionally—in the gallery of all those who, from one end of the book to the other, announce, like heralds of good tidings, the very possibility of the book: above all Nietzsche and, most frequently, Nietzsche and Artaud, who are often associated in the same sentence—Nietzsche, Artaud, Van Gogh, sometimes Nerval, and Hölderlin from time to time. Their excess, "the madness in which the work of art is engulfed," is the gulf or abyss out of which opens "the space of our enterprise" (*M*, p. 288; *F*, p. 643).

It is *before* this madness, in the fleeting moment when it is joined to the work, that we are *responsible*. We are far from being able to arraign it or make it appear, for it is we who must appear *before* it. Let us recognize, then, that we are responsible before it rather than being authorized to examine it [*arraisonner*], to objectify and demand an explanation from it. At the end of the last page, after having spent a good deal of time speaking of Nietzsche and after having mentioned Van Gogh, Foucault writes: "The moment when, together, the work of art and madness are born and fulfilled is the beginning of the time when the world finds itself arraigned by that work of art and responsible before it for what it is" (*M*, p. 289; *F*, p. 643). This is, in sum, what *The History of Madness*, in responding to the summons, takes note of and assumes responsibility for. It assumes responsibility before that which is named by the names of Nietzsche and all these others who, as everyone knows, were deemed crazy by society (Artaud, and before him Van Gogh, and before him Nerval, and before him Hölderlin).

But what about Freud? Why is he, in the same book, sometimes associated with and sometimes opposed to these great witnesses of madness and excess, these great witnesses who are also great judges, our judges, those who judge us? Must we be arraigned before Freud? And why do things then get complicated?

I would see the chiasmus of which I just spoke in a place where Freud is in fact found near Nietzsche, on the same side as he, that is, on our side, on the side of what Foucault calls "contemporary man": this enigmatic "we" for whom a history of madness opens today, cracks open the door of today [*l'huis d'aujourd'hui*] so that its possibility may be glimpsed. Foucault has just described the loss of unreason, the background against which the classical age determined madness. It is the moment when unreason degenerates or disappears into the unreasonable; it is the tendency to pathologize, so to speak, madness. And there again, it is through a return to unreason, this time without exclusion, that Nietzsche and Freud reopen the dialogue with madness *itself* (assuming, along with Foucault, that one can here say "itself"). This dialogue had, in a sense, been broken off twice, and in two different ways: the second time by yesterday's psychological positivism, which no longer conceived of madness as unreason; the first time by the classical age,

which, while excluding madness and breaking off the dialogue with
it, still determined it as unreason and excluded it precisely because
of this—but excluded it as close as possible to itself, as its other and
its adversary. The latter is the Cartesian moment, such as it is
determined, at least, in the three pages that were the object of our
debate nearly thirty years ago.

I will underscore everything that marks the *today,* the present,
the now, the contemporary, this time that is proper and common to
us, the time of this fragile and divided "we" from which is decided
the possibility of a book like *The History of Madness,* decided while
scarcely being sketched out, while promising itself, in short, rather
than giving itself over. Nietzsche *and* Freud are conjoined, conju-
gated, like a couple, Nietzsche *and* Freud, and the conjunction of
their coupling is also the copula-hinge or, if you prefer, the middle
term of the modern proposition:

> If *contemporary* man, since Nietzsche and Freud, finds deep within
> himself the site for contesting all truth, being able to read, in what he
> *now* knows of himself, the signs of fragility through which unreason
> threatens, seventeenth-century man, on the contrary, discovers, in the
> immediate presence of his thought to itself, the certainty in which
> reason in its pure form is announced. (*F,* pp. 195–96)

2. The Evil Genius—of the Chiasmus

Why did I speak of a chiasmus? And why would we be fascinated
by the multiple chiasmus that organizes this entire interpretative
scene?

It is because, in the three pages devoted to Descartes at the
beginning of the second chapter, "The Great Confinement,"
Foucault spoke of an *exclusion.* He described it, posed it, declared it
unequivocally and firmly ("madness is excluded by the subject who
doubts"). This exclusion was the result of a "decision," the result
(and these are all his words) of a "strange act of force" that was
going to "reduce to silence" the excluded madness and trace a very
strict "line of division." In the part of the *Meditations* that he cited

and focused on, Foucault left out all mention of the Evil Genius. It was thus in recalling the hyperbolic raising of the stakes in the fiction of the Evil Genius that I then confessed my perplexity and proposed other questions. When Foucault responds to me nine years later in the afterword to the 1972 Gallimard edition of *The History of Madness*, he still firmly contests the way I used this Cartesian fiction of the Evil Genius and this hyperbolic moment of doubt. He accuses me of erasing "everything that shows that the episode of the evil genius is an exercise that is voluntary, controlled, mastered, and carried out from start to finish by a meditating subject who never lets himself be surprised" (*F*, p. 601).[10] (Such a reproach was indeed unfair, unjust, since I had stressed that this methodical mastery of the voluntary subject is "almost always" at work and that Foucault, therefore, like Descartes, is "almost always right [*a . . . raison*]," and almost always wins out over [*a raison de*] the Evil Genius.[11] But that is not what is at issue here, and I said that I would not reopen the debate.) By accusing me of erasing this methodical neutralization of the Evil Genius, Foucault—once again in his response of 1972—confirms the claims of the three pages in question and maintains that "if the evil genius again takes on the powers of *madness*, this is only after the exercise of medita-tion has excluded the risk of *being mad*."[12] One might be tempted to respond that if the Evil Genius can *again take on* these powers of madness, if he once "again takes them on" afterwards, after the fact, it is because the exclusion of the risk of being mad makes way for an *after*. The narrative is thus not interrupted during the exclusion alleged by Foucault, an exclusion that is, up to a certain point at least, attested to and incontestable (and I never in fact contested this exclusion in this regard, quite the contrary); neither the narra-tive nor the exercise of the meditation that it retraces are any more interrupted than the order of reasons is definitively stopped by this same exclusion. But let us move on. As I said earlier, I am not invoking this difficulty in order to return to an old discussion. I am doing it because Freud is going to be, as I will try to show, doubly situated, *twice* implicated in the chiasmus that interests me. *On the one hand*, the sentence that I cited a moment ago (where Freud was immediately associated with Nietzsche, the only one to be associated with him, on the "good" side, so to speak, on the side where "we" contemporaries reopen the dialogue with unreason that was twice interrupted) is followed by a few references to the Evil Genius that complicate, as I myself had tried to do, the reading of the scene of Cartesian doubt as the moment of the great confinement. *On the other hand*, I will later try, in a more indirect way—and this will be the essence of my talk today—to recall the necessity of taking into account a certain Evil Genius *of* Freud, namely, the presence of the demonic, the devil, the devil's advocate, the limping devil, and so on in *Beyond the Pleasure Principle*, where psychoanalysis finds, it seems to me, its greatest speculative power but also the place of greatest resistance *to* psychoanalysis (death drive, repetition compulsion, and so on, and *fort/da!*).

Thus, just after having spoken of "contemporary man, since Nietzsche and Freud," Foucault offers a development *on the subject of the Evil Genius*. The logic of this sequence seems to me guided by a "one must not forget" that I would be tempted to relate to the "one must do justice" of a moment ago. What must one not forget? The Evil Genius, of course [*justement*]. And especially, I emphasize, the fact that the Evil Genius is *anterior* to the cogito, so that its threat remains *perpetual*.

This might contradict (as I had attempted to do) the thesis argued 150 pages earlier on the subject of the Cartesian cogito as the simple exclusion of madness. This could have, as a result, indeed this *should* have, spared us a long and dramatic debate. But it is too late now. Foucault reaffirms all the same, despite the recognized anteriority of the Evil Genius, that the cogito is the absolute beginning, even if, in this absolute beginning, "one must not forget" what has, in short, been forgotten or omitted in the discourse on the exclusion of madness by the cogito. The question thus still remains what a methodically absolute beginning would be that does not let us forget this anterior—and, moreover, perpetual—threat, nor the *haunting* backdrop that first lets it appear. As always, I prefer to cite, even though it is a long passage. Here is what Foucault says immediately after having evoked the "contemporary man" who "since Nietzsche and Freud," meets in "what he now knows of himself" that "through which unreason threatens." He says, in effect, that what is called contemporary had already begun in the classical age and with the Evil Genius, which clearly, to my eyes at least, cannot leave intact the historical categories of reference and the presumed identity of something like the "classical age" (for example).

> But this does not mean that classical man was, in his experience of the truth, more distanced from unreason than we ourselves might be. It is true that the cogito is the absolute beginning [this statement thus confirms the thesis of *F*, pp. 54–57] *but one must not forget* [my emphasis] that the evil genius is anterior to it. And the evil genius is not the symbol in which are summed up and systematized all the dangers of such psychological events as dream images and sensory errors. Between God and man, the evil genius has an absolute meaning: he is in all his rigor the possibility of unreason and the totality of its powers. He is more than the refraction of human finitude; well beyond man, he signals the danger that could prevent man once and for all from gaining access to the truth: he is the main obstacle, not of such a spirit but of such reason. And it is not because the truth that gets illuminated in the cogito ends up entirely masking the shadow of the evil genius that one *ought to forget* its perpetually threatening power [my emphasis: Foucault had earlier said that *one must not forget* that the evil genius is anterior to the cogito, and he now says that *one must not forget* its perpetually threatening power, even after the passage, the moment, the experience, the certainty of the cogito, and the exclusion of madness that this brings about]: this danger will hover over Descartes' reflections right up until the establishment of the existence and truth of the external world. (*F*, p. 196)

One may imagine the effects that the category of the "perpetual threat" (Foucault's term) can have on indications of presence, positive markings, the determinations made by means of signs or statements, in short, the whole criteriology and symptomatology that can give assurance to a historical knowledge concerning a figure, an *episteme*, an age, an epoch, a paradigm, once all these determinations are found to be *threatened*, and *perpetually* so, perpetually disturbed by a haunting. In principle, all these determinations are, for the historian, either presences or absences. They *exclude haunting*. They allow themselves to be located by means of signs, one would almost say on a table of absences and presences; they come out of the logic of opposition, in this case, the logic of inclusion *or* exclusion, of the alternative between the inside and the outside, and so on. The perpetual threat, that is, the shadow of haunting (and haunting is, like the phantom or fiction of an Evil Genius, neither present nor absent, neither positive nor negative, neither inside nor outside), does not challenge only one thing or another; it threatens the logic that distinguishes between one thing and another, the very logic of exclusion or foreclosure, as well as the history that is founded upon this logic and its alternatives. What is excluded is, of course, never simply excluded, neither by the cogito nor by anything else, without this eventually returning—and that is what a certain psychoanalysis will have also helped us to understand. Let me leave undeveloped this general problem, however, in order to return to a certain regulated functioning in the references to psychoanalysis and to the name of Freud in *The History of Madness in the Classical Age*.

Let us consider the couple Nietzsche/Freud, this *odd couple* about which there is so much else to say (I have attempted this elsewhere, especially in *The Post Card*, and precisely [*justement*] in relationship to *Beyond the Pleasure Principle*). The affiliation or filiation of this couple reappears elsewhere. It is again at a filial limit, in the introduction to the third and final part, when the "delirium" of *Rameau's Nephew* sets the tone or gives the key, just as the Cartesian cogito had, for a new arrangement or division [*partition*]. The "delirium" of *Rameau's Nephew*, writes Foucault, "announces Freud and Nietzsche." Let us set aside all the questions that the concept of "announcing" might pose for the historian. Not by accident do they resemble those raised a moment ago by the concept of *haunting*. As soon as that which *announces* no longer completely belongs to a present configuration and already belongs to the future of another, its place, the taking-place of its event, calls for another logic; it disturbs, in any case, the axiomatics of a history that places too much trust in the opposition between absence and presence, outside and inside, inclusion and exclusion. Let us read, then, this sentence and note the recurring (recurrence counts) and thus all the more striking association of this *announcement* with the figure of the Evil Genius, but, this time, with the figure of "another evil genius": "The delirium of Rameau's Nephew is a tragic confrontation of need and illusion in an oneiric mode, one that announces Freud and Nietzsche [the order of names is this time reversed]; it is also the ironic repetition of the world, its destructive reconstitution in the theater of illusion" (*F,* p. 422).

An Evil Genius then immediately reappears. And who will see this inevitable repetition as a coincidence? But it is not the same Evil Genius. It is another figure of the Evil Genius. There would thus be a recurring function of the Evil Genius, a function that, in making reference to a Platonic *hyperbole,* I called hyperbolic in "Cogito and the History of Madness." This function was fulfilled by the Evil Genius, under the guise as well as under the name that it takes on in Descartes. But another Evil Genius, which is also the same one, can reappear without this name and under a different guise, for example, in the vicinity or lineage of Rameau's Nephew: a different Evil Genius, certainly, but bearing enough of a resemblance because of its recurring function that the historian, here Foucault, allows himself a metonymy that is legitimate enough in his eyes to continue calling it Evil Genius. This re-apparition occurs after the second passage of Freud-and-Nietzsche, as they are furtively announced by *Rameau's Nephew,* whose laugh "prefigures in advance and reduces the whole movement of nineteenth-century anthropology" (*F,* p. 424). This time of prefiguration and announcement, this delay between the anticipatory lightning flash and the event of what is foreseen, is explained by the very structure of an experience of unreason, if there is any, namely, an experience in which one cannot maintain oneself and out of which one cannot but fall after having approached it. All this thus forbids our making this history into a properly successive and sequential history of events. This is formulated in Foucault's question: "Why is it

not possible to maintain oneself in the difference of unreason?"
(*F*, p. 425).

But in this vertigo where the truth of the world is maintained only on
the inside of an absolute void, man also encounters the ironic perver-
sion of his own truth, at the moment when it moves from the dreams
of interiority to the forms of exchange. Unreason then takes on the
figure of *another evil genius* [my emphasis]—no longer the one who
exiles man from the truth of the world, but the one who at once
mystifies and demystifies, enchants to the point of extreme disen-
chantment, this truth of man that man had entrusted to his hands, to
his face, to his speech; an evil genius who no longer operates when
man wants to accede to the truth but when he wants to restitute to the
world a truth that is his own, when, thrown into the intoxication of
the sensible realm where he is lost, he finally remains "immobile,
stupid, astonished." It is no longer in *perception* that the possibility
of the evil genius resides [that is, as in Descartes] but in *expression*.
(*F*, p. 423)

But immediately after this appearance or arraignment of Freud
next to Nietzsche and all the Evil Geniuses, the pendulum of the
fort/da is put in motion: from this point on, it will not cease to
convoke and dismiss Freud from the two sides of the dividing line,
both inside and outside of the series that puts its signature to the
history of madness. For it is here, in the following pages, that we
find Freud separated from the lineage in which are gathered all
those worthy heirs of Rameau's Nephew. The name of the one who
was not crazy, not crazy enough in any case, the name of Freud, is
dissociated from that of Nietzsche. It is regularly passed over in
silence when, according to another filiation, Hölderlin, Nerval,
Nietzsche, Van Gogh, Roussel, and Artaud are at several reprieves
named and renamed—renowned—within the same "family."

From this point on, things get worse. "To do justice to Freud"
will more and more come to mean putting on trial a psychoanalysis
that will have participated, in its own way, however original that
may be, in the order of the immemorial figures of the Father and
the Judge, of Family and Law, in the order of Order, of Authority

and Punishment, whose immemorial figures must, as Philippe Pinel noted, be brought into play by the doctor, in order to cure (see *M*, p. 272; *F*, p. 607). There was already a disturbing sign of this long before the chapter "The Birth of the Asylum," which strictly inscribes psychoanalysis into the tradition of Tuke and Pinel and goes so far as to say that "all nineteenth-century psychiatry really converges on Freud" (*M*, p. 277; *F*, p. 611). Freud had already appeared in another chain, the chain of those who, since the nineteenth century, know that madness, like its counterpart reason, has a history. These will have even been led astray by a sort of historicism of reason and madness, a risk that is avoided by those who, "from Sade to Hölderlin, to Nerval and to Nietzsche," are given over to a "repeated poetic and philosophical experience" and plunge into a language "that abolishes history." Being a cultural historian of madness, as others are of reason, Freud thus appears between Janet and Brunschvicg (*F*, p. 456).

While accumulating the two errors, Freud as rationalist historian of this cultural phenomenon called madness nonetheless continues to pay tribute to myth, magic, and thaumaturgy. Indeed *thaumaturgy* will be the word chosen by Foucault himself for the verdict. There is nothing surprising in this collusion of reason and a certain occultism. Montaigne and Pascal would have perhaps called it mystical or secret authority; the history of reason and reason within history would exercise essentially the same violence, the same obscure, irrational, dictatorial violence, serving the same interests in the name of the same fictional allegation, as psychoanalysis does when it confers all powers to the doctor's speech. Freud would free the patient interned in the asylum only to reconstitute him "in his essential character" at the heart of the analytic situation. There is a continuity from Pinel and Tuke to psychoanalysis. There is an inevitable movement, right up to Freud, a persistence of what Foucault calls "the myth of Pinel, like that of Tuke" (*F*, p. 577). This insistence is always concentrated in the figure of the doctor; it is, in the eyes of the patient, who is always an accomplice, the becoming-thaumaturge of the doctor, of

a doctor who is not even supposed to know. *Homo medicus* does not
exercise his authority in the name of science but, as Pinel himself
seems to recognize and to claim, in the name of order, law, and
morality, specifically, by "relying upon that prestige that envelops
the *secrets* of the Family, of Authority, of Punishment, and of
Love; . . . by wearing the mask of Father and of Judge" (*M*, p. 273;
F, pp. 607–8; my emphasis).

3. The Other Secret of Psychoanalysis: The "Mystical Foundation of Authority"

When the walls of the asylum give way to psychoanalysis, a
certain concept of the *secret* maintains the tradition from Pinel to
Freud. It would be necessary to follow throughout these pages all
the ins and outs of the value—itself barely visible—of a secret, of a
certain secrecy value. This value would come down, in the end, to a
technique of the secret, and of the secret without knowledge. Wherever knowledge can only be supposed, wherever, as a result, one
knows that supposition cannot give rise to knowledge, wherever no
knowledge could ever be disputed, there is the invisible production
(for no one ever witnesses it) of a *secrecy effect*, of what we might call
a *speculation on the capital secret or on the capital of the secret*. The
calculated and yet finally incalculable production of this secrecy
effect relies on a simulacrum. This simulacrum recalls, from another point of view, the situation described at the opening of
Raymond Roussel: the risk of "being deceived less by a secret than by
the awareness that there is a secret."[13]

What persists from Pinel to Freud, in spite of all the differences,
is the figure of the doctor as a man not of knowledge but of order.
In this figure all *secret, magic, esoteric, thaumaturgical* powers are
brought together—and these are all Foucault's words. The scientific
objectivity that is claimed by this tradition is only a magical
reification:

> If we wanted to analyze the profound structures of objectivity in the
> knowledge and practice of nineteenth-century psychiatry from Pinel

to Freud [this is the definitive divorce between Nietzsche and Freud, the second coupling for the latter], we should have to show in fact that such objectivity was from the start a reification of a magical nature, which could only be accomplished with the complicity of the patient himself, and beginning from a transparent and clear moral practice, gradually forgotten as positivism imposed its myths of scientific objectivity. (*M*, p. 276; *F*, p. 610)

In the name of Freud, one can read the call for a note. At the bottom of the page, Foucault confirms, dates, and signs, but the note introduces a slight precaution. It is indeed a note of prudence, but Foucault insists nonetheless and speaks of persistence: "These structures still persist in non-psychoanalytic psychiatry, and in many aspects or on many sides [*par bien des côtés*] of psychoanalysis itself" (*M*, p. 299; *F*, p. 610).

There is indeed a limit, though too discreetly marked, to what persists "on many sides." The always divisible line of this limit situates, in its form, the totality of the stakes. More precisely, the stakes are nothing other than those of *totality*, and of the procedures of *totalization*: What does it mean to say psychoanalysis "itself"? What does one thereby identify in such a global way? Is it psychoanalysis "itself," as Foucault says, that inherits from Pinel? What is psychoanalysis *itself*? And are the aspects or sides through which it inherits the essential and irreducible aspects or sides of psychoanalysis itself or the residual "asides" that it can win out over [*avoir raison de*]? or even, that it must, that it should, win out over?

If in this note the answer to this last question still seems up in the air, it will soon come in a more determined and less equivocal form: no, psychoanalysis will never free itself from the psychiatric heritage. Its essential historical situation is linked to what is called the "analytic situation," that is, to the thaumaturgical mystification of the couple doctor-patient, regulated this time by institutional protocols. Before citing word for word a conclusion that will remain, I believe, without appeal not only in *The History of Madness* but in Foucault's entire oeuvre—right up to its awful interruption—I will once again abuse your patience in order to look for a moment at the way in which Foucault describes the thaumaturgical play whose *technē* Pinel would have passed down to Freud, a *technē* that would be at once art and technique, the secret, the secret of the secret, the secret that consists in knowing how to make one suppose knowledge and believe in the secret. It is worth pausing here in order to point out another paradoxical effect of the chiasmus—one of the most significant for what concerns us here, namely, a certain diabolical repetition and the recurrence of the various figures of the Evil Genius.

What does Foucault say? That in the couple doctor-patient "the doctor becomes a thaumaturge" (*M*, p. 275; *F*, p. 609). Now, to describe this thaumaturgy, Foucault does not hesitate to speak of the demonic and satanic, as if the Evil Genius resided this time not on the side of unreason, of absolute disorder and madness (to say it quickly and with a bit of a smile, using all the necessary quotation marks, "on the good side"), but on the side of order, on the side of a subtly authoritative violence, the side of the Father, the Judge, the Law, and so on:

> It was thought, and by the patient first of all, that it was in the esotericism of his knowledge, in some *almost* daemonic secret of knowledge [I emphasize "almost": Foucault will later say—his relation to Freud surely being anything but simple—that the philistine representation of mental illness in the nineteenth century would last "right up to Freud—or almost"] that the doctor had found the power to unravel insanity; and increasingly the patient would accept this self-surrender to a doctor both divine and satanic, beyond human measure in any case. (*M*, p. 275; *F*, p. 609)

Two pages later, it is said that Freud "amplified the thaumaturgical virtues" of the "medical personage," "preparing for his omnipotence a quasi-divine status." Foucault continues:

> He focussed upon this single presence—concealed behind the patient and above him, in an absence that is also a total presence—all the powers that had been distributed in the collective existence of the asylum; he transformed this into an absolute Observation, a pure and circumspect Silence, a Judge who punishes and rewards in a judgment

that does not even condescend to language; he made it the mirror in which madness, in an almost motionless movement, clings to and casts off itself.

To the doctor, Freud transferred all the structures Pinel and Tuke had set up within confinement. (*M*, pp. 277–78; *F*, p. 611)

Fictive omnipotence and a divine, or rather "quasi-divine," power, divine by simulacrum, at once divine and satanic—these are the very traits of an Evil Genius, which are now being attributed to the figure of the doctor. The doctor suddenly begins to resemble in a troubling way the figure of unreason that continued to haunt what is called the classical age after the *act of force* [coup de force] of the *cogito*. And like the authority of the laws whose "mystical founda-tion" is recalled by Montaigne and Pascal,[14] the authority of the psychoanalyst-doctor is but the effect of a fiction; it proceeds, by transfer, from the credit given to a fiction; and this fiction appears analogous to that which provisionally confers all powers—and even more than knowledge—to the Evil Genius.

At the conclusion of "The Birth of the Asylum," Foucault dismisses without appeal this bad genius of the thaumaturgical doctor in the figure of the psychoanalyst; he does this—I believe one can say without stretching the paradox—*against Descartes*, against a certain Cartesian subject still represented in the filiation that runs from Descartes to Pinel to Freud. But he also does this, more or less willingly, *as Descartes*, or, at least, as the Descartes whom he had accused of excluding madness by excluding, master-ing, or dismissing—since these all come down to the same thing— the powers of the Evil Genius. Against Freud, this descendant of Descartes, against Descartes, it is still the Cartesian exclusion that is repeated in a deadly and devilish way, like a heritage inscribed within a diabolical and almost all-powerful program that one should admit one never gets rid of or frees oneself from without remainder.

To substantiate what I have just said, I will cite the conclusion of this chapter. It describes the transfer from Pinel to Freud (stroke of genius, "masterful short-circuit"—it is a question of Freud's genius, the good like the bad, the good *as* bad)—and it implacably judges psychoanalysis *in the past, in the present, and even in the future. For psychoanalysis is condemned in advance.* No future is promised to it that might allow it to escape its destiny once it has been determined both within the institutional (and supposedly inflexible) structure of what is called the *analytic situation* and in the figure of the doctor as *subject*:

> To the doctor, Freud transferred all the structures Pinel and Tuke had set up within confinement. He did deliver the patient from the existence of the asylum within which his "liberators" had alienated him; but he did not deliver him from what was essential in this existence; he regrouped its powers, extended them to the maximum by uniting them in the doctor's hands; he created the psychoanalytical situation where, by a masterful short-circuit [*court-circuit génial*; I underscore this allusion to the stroke of genius (*coup de génie*), which, as soon as it confirms the evil of confinement and of the interior asylum, is diabolical and properly evil (*malin*); and as we will see, for more than twenty years Foucault never stopped seeing in Freud—and quite literally so—sometimes a good and sometimes a bad or evil (*mauvais*) genius], alienation becomes disalienating because, in the doctor, it becomes a subject.
>
> The doctor, as an alienating figure, remains the key to psychoanalysis. It is perhaps because it did not suppress this ultimate structure, and because it referred all the others to it, that psychoanalysis has not been able, *will not be able* [I emphasize this future; it announces the invariability of this verdict in Foucault's subsequent work], to hear the voices of unreason, nor to decipher in themselves the signs of the madman. Psychoanalysis can unravel some of the forms of madness; it remains a stranger to the sovereign enterprise of unreason. It can neither liberate nor transcribe, nor most certainly explain, what is essential in this enterprise. (*M*, p. 278; *F*, pp. 611–12)

And here, just after, are the very last lines of the chapter; we are far from the couple Nietzsche/Freud. They are now separated on both sides of what Foucault calls "moral imprisonment," and it will always be difficult to say, in certain situations, who is to be found on the *inside* and who on the *outside*—and sometimes outside but inside. As opposed to Nietzsche and a few other great madmen, Freud no longer belongs to the space *out of* which *The History of Madness* could be written. He belongs, rather, to the history of madness that the book makes its *object*:

> Since the end of the eighteenth century, the life of unreason no longer manifests itself except in the lightning-flash of works such as those of Hölderlin, of Nerval, of Neitzsche, or of Artaud—forever irreducible to those alienations that can be cured, resisting by their own strength that gigantic moral imprisonment which we are in the habit of calling, doubtless by antiphrasis, the liberation of the insane [*aliénés*] by Pinel and Tuke. (*M*, p. 278; *F*, p. 612)

This diagnosis, which is also a verdict, is confirmed in the last chapter of the book, "The Anthropological Circle." This chapter fixes the new distribution of names and places into the great series that form the grid of the book. When it comes to showing that since the end of the eighteenth century the liberation of the mad has been replaced by an objectification of the concept of their freedom (within such categories as desire and will, determinism and responsibility, the automatic and the spontaneous) and that "one will now untiringly recount the trials and tribulations of freedom," which is also to say, of a certain humanization as anthropologization, Freud is then regularly included among the exemplary figures of this anthropologism of freedom. Foucault says, page after page: "From Esquirol to Janet, as from Reil to Freud or from Tuke to Jackson" (*F*, p. 616), or again, "from Esquirol to Freud" (*F*, p. 617), or again "from Esquirol and Broussais right up to Janet, Bleuler, and Freud" (*F*, p. 624). A slight yet troubling reservation comes just after to mitigate all these regroupings: it is yet another "almost." Concerning general paralysis and neurosyphilis, philistinism is everywhere, "right up to Freud—or almost" (*F*, p. 626).

The chiasmatic effects multiply. Some two hundred pages earlier, what inscribes both Freud *and* Nietzsche, like two accomplices of the same age, is the reopening of the dialogue with unreason, the lifting of the interdiction against *language*, the *return* to a proximity with madness. Yet it is precisely this or, rather, the silent double and hypocritical simulacrum of this, the mask of this language, the same freedom now objectified, that separates Freud from Nietzsche. It is this that now makes them unable to associate or to be associated with one another from the two sides of a wall that is all the more insurmountable insofar as it consists of an asylum's partition, an invisible, interior, but eloquent partition, that of truth itself as the truth of man and his alienation. Foucault was able, much earlier, to say that Freudian psychoanalysis, to which one must be fair or "*do justice,*" is not a psychology as soon as it takes language into account. Now it is language itself that brings psychoanalysis back down to the status of a psycho-anthropology of alienation, "this language wherein man appears in madness as being other than himself," this "alterity," "a dialectic that is always begun anew between the *Same* and the *Other,*" revealing to man his truth "in the babbling movement of *alienation* or *madness*" (*F,* p. 631).

As concerns dialectic and alienation or madness—as concerns everything, in fact, that happens in the circulation of this "anthropological circle" wherein psychoanalysis is caught up or held—one should pause a bit longer than Foucault did on a passage from Hegel's *Encyclopedia.* I am referring to the Remark of §408 in which Hegel situates and deduces madness as a contradiction of the subject between the particular determination of self-feeling and the network of mediations that is called consciousness. Hegel makes in passing a spirited praise of Pinel (I do not understand why Foucault, in quickly citing this passage, replaces this praise for Pinel by an ellipsis). More important, Hegel also interprets madness as a certain Evil Genius (*der böse Genius*) taking control in man. Foucault elliptically cites a short phrase in translation ("méchant génie") without remarking on it and without linking these few extraordinary pages of Hegel to the great dramaturgy of the Evil Genius that concerns us here.

Let me be quite clear about this: my intention here is not at all to accuse or criticize Foucault, to say, for example, that he was wrong to confine *Freud himself* (*in general*) or *psychoanalysis itself* (*in general*) to this role and place; on the subject of Freud or psychoanalysis *themselves and in general*, I have in this form and place almost nothing to say or think, except perhaps that Foucault has some good arguments and that others would have some pretty good ones as well to oppose to his. It is also not my intention, however it may seem, to suggest that Foucault contradicts himself when he so firmly places the same Freud (in general) or the same psychoanalysis (in general) sometimes on one side and sometimes on the other of the dividing line, and always on the side of the Evil Genius—who is found sometimes on the side of madness, sometimes on the side of its exclusion-reappropriation, on the side of its confinement to the outside or the inside, with or without asylum walls. The contradiction is no doubt in the things themselves, so to speak. And we are in a region where the wrong (the *being-wrong* or the *doing-someone-wrong*) would want to be more than ever on the side of a certain reason, on the side of what is called *raison garder*—that is, on the side of keeping one's cool, keeping one's head—on the side, precisely, where one is right [*a raison*], and where *being right* [avoir raison] is to *win out over* or *prove someone wrong* [avoir raison de], with a violence whose subtlety, whose hyperdialectic and hyperchiasmatic resources, cannot be completely formalized, that is, can no longer be dominated by a metalanguage. Which means that we are always caught in the knots that are woven, before us and beyond us, by this powerful—all too powerful—logic. The history of reason embedded in all these turbulent idioms (*to prove someone wrong* [donner tort] or *to prove them right* [donner raison], *to be right* [avoir raison], *to be wrong* [avoir tort], *to win out over* [avoir raison de], *to do someone wrong* [faire tort], and so on) is also the history of madness that Foucault wished to recount to us. The fact that he was caught up, caught up even before setting out, in the snares of this logic—which he sometimes thematizes as having to do with a "system of contradictions" and "antinomies" whose "coherence" remains "hidden"—cannot be reduced to a fault or wrong on his part (*F,* p. 624). This does not mean, however, that we, without ever finding him to be radically wrong or at fault, have to subscribe *a priori* to all his statements. One would be able to master this entire problematic, assuming this were possible, only after having satisfactorily answered a few questions, questions as innocent as What is reason?, for example, or, more narrowly, What is the principle of reason? What does it mean to be right [*avoir raison*]? What does it mean to be right or to prove someone right [*avoir ou donner raison*]? To be wrong, to prove someone wrong, or to do them wrong [*avoir, donner ou faire tort*]? You will forgive me here, I hope, for leaving these enigmas as they are.

4. The "Stroke of Genius": A Tireless *Fort/Da*

I will restrict myself to a modest and more accessible question. The distribution of statements, as it appears to be set out before us, should lead us to think two apparently incompatible things: the book entitled *The History of Madness*, like the history of madness itself, is and is not the same age as Freudian psychoanalysis. The project of this book thus does and does not belong to the age of psychoanalysis; it already belongs to it and already no longer belongs to it. This division without division would put us back on the track of another logic of division, one that would urge us to think the internal partitions of wholes, partitions that would make such things as madness, reason, history, and age—especially the whole we call "age"—but also psychoanalysis, Freud, and so on into rather dubious identities, sufficiently divided from within to threaten in advance all our statements and all our references with parasitism: it would be a bit as if a virus were introduced into the matrix of language, the way such things are today introduced into computer software, the difference being that we are—and for a very good reason—very far from having at our disposal any of the diagnostic and remedial antiviral programs that are available on the market today, even though these programs—and for a very good reason—have a hard time keeping pace with the industrial production of these viruses, which are themselves sometimes produced by those who produce the intercepting programs. A maddening situation for any discourse, certainly, but a certain mad panic is not necessarily the worst thing that can happen to a discourse on madness as soon as it does not go all out to confine or exclude its object, that is, in the sense Foucault gives to this word, to *objectify* it.

Does one have the right to stop here and be content with this as an internal reading of Foucault's great book? Is an *internal* reading possible? Is it legitimate to privilege to this extent its relation to something like an "age" of psychoanalysis "itself"? The reservations that such presumptions of identity might arouse (the unity of an "age," the indivisibility of psychoanalysis "itself," and so on— and I've made more than one allusion to them) would be enough to make us question this.

One could justify a response to this question only by continuing to read and to analyze, by continuing to take into account in particular Foucault's corpus, his archive, what this archive says on the subject of the archive. Without limiting ourselves to this, think of the problems posed some five to eight years later: (1) by *The Order of Things* concerning something that has always seemed enigmatic to me and that Foucault calls for a time *episteme* (there where it is said, "We think in that place" [*OT*, p. 384; *MC*, p. 396]); a place that, and I will return to this in a moment, encompasses or comprehends the psychoanalysis that does not comprehend it, or more precisely, that comprehends it without comprehending it and without acceding to it; (2) by *The Archaeology of Knowledge* concerning "The Historical *a priori* and the Archive" (the title of a central chapter) and archaeology in its relation to the history of ideas.

It is out of the question to get involved here in such difficult readings. I will thus be content to conclude, if you will still allow me, with a few indications (two at the most) along one of the paths I would have wanted to follow in these readings.

1. *The pendulum, death, and us.* One the one hand, I would have tried to identify the signs of an imperturbable constancy in the movement of the pendulum or balance. The oscillation *regularly* leads from one topological assignation to the other: as if psychoanalysis had *two places* or took place *two times, two times at the same*

time. Yet it seems to me that the law of this displacement operates without the structural possibility of an event or a place being analyzed for itself, and without the consequences being drawn with regard to the identity of all the concepts at work in this history that does not want to be a history of ideas and representations.

This constancy in the oscillation of the pendulum is first marked, of course, in books that are more or less contemporary with *The History of Madness. Maladie mentale et psychologie* (*Mental Illness and Psychology*; 1962) intersects and coincides at many points with *The History of Madness.* In the history of mental illness, Freud appears as "the first to open up once again the possibility for reason and unreason to communicate in the danger of a common language, ever ready to break down and disintegrate into the inaccessible" (*MI,* p. 69; *MM,* p. 82). In truth, though profoundly in accord with the movement and logic of *The History of Madness,* this book of 1962 is, in the end, a bit more precise and differentiated in its references to Freud, although *Beyond the Pleasure Principle* is never mentioned. Foucault speaks both of Freud's "stroke of genius" (this is indeed his word) and of the dividing line that runs through his work. Freud's "stroke of genius" was to have escaped the evolutionist horizon of John Hughlings Jackson (*MI,* p. 31; *MM,* p. 37), whose model can nevertheless be found in the description of the evolutionary forms of neurosis and the history of libidinal stages,[15] the libido being mythological (a myth to destroy, often a biopsychological myth that is abandoned, Foucault then thinks, by psychoanalysts), just as mythological as Janet's "'psychic force,'" with which Foucault associates it more than once (*MI,* p. 24; *MM,* p. 29).[16]

If the assignation of Freud is thus double, it is because his work is divided: "In psychoanalysis, it is always possible," says Foucault, "to separate that which pertains to a psychology of evolution (as in *Three Essays on the Theory of Sexuality*) and that which belongs to a psychology of individual history (as in *Five Psychoanalyses* and the accompanying texts)" (*MI,* p. 31; *MM,* p. 37).

Despite this consideration for the "stroke of genius," Foucault is speaking here of an analytic psychology. This is what he calls it.

Insofar as it remains a psychology, it remains speechless before the language of madness. Indeed, "there is a very good reason why psychology can never master madness; it is because psychology became possible in our world only when madness had already been mastered and excluded from the drama" (*MI*, p. 87; *MM*, p. 104—a few lines before the end of the book).

The excess of mastery ruins mastery. In other words, the logic at work in this conclusion, whose—ruinous—consequences one would ceaselessly have to take into account, is that what has already been mastered can no longer be mastered, and that too much mastery (in the form of exclusion but also of objectification) deprives one of mastery (in the form of access, knowledge, competence). The concept of mastery is an impossible concept to manipulate, as we know: the more there is, the less there is, and vice versa. The conclusion drawn in the few lines I just cited thus excludes *both* Freud's "stroke of genius" *and* psychology, be it analytic or some other. Freudian man remains a *homo psychologicus*. Freud is once again passed over in silence, cut out of both the lineage and the work of mad geniuses. He is sent back to oblivion, where one can then accuse him of silence and forgetting.

> And when in lightning flashes and cries, madness reappears, as in Nerval or Artaud, Nietzsche or Roussel, it is psychology that remains silent, *speechless* [Foucault's emphasis], before this language that borrows a meaning of its own from that *tragic split* [I emphasize this phrase; this is a tragic and romantic discourse on the essence of madness and the birth of tragedy, a discourse just as close, literally, to that of a certain Novalis as to that of Hölderlin], from that freedom that, for contemporary man, only the existence of "psychologists" allows him to forget. (*MI*, pp. 87–88; *MM*, p. 104)[17]

And yet. Still according to the interminable and inexhaustible *fort/da*, which we have been following for some time now, the same *Freudian man* is reinscribed into the noble lineage at the end of *Naissance de la clinique* (*The Birth of the Clinic*; a book published in 1963 but clearly written out of the same impulse). Why single out this occurrence of the reinscription rather than another? Because it might give us (this is the hypothesis that interests me) a rule for reading this *fort/da*; it might provide us with a criterion for interpreting this untiring exclusion/inclusion. It is a question of another divide, within psychoanalysis, a divide that seems somewhat different from the one I spoke of a moment ago between Freud the psychologist of evolution and Freud the psychologist of individual history. I say "seems somewhat different" because the one perhaps leads back to the other.

The line of this second divide is, quite simply—if one can say this—death. The Freud who breaks with psychology, with evolutionism and biologism, the tragic Freud, really, who shows himself *hospitable* to madness (and I risk this word) because he is foreign to the space of the hospital, the tragic Freud who deserves hospitality in the great lineage of mad geniuses, is the Freud who talks it out with death. This would especially be the Freud, then, of *Beyond the Pleasure Principle*, although Foucault *never*, to my knowledge, mentions this work and makes only a very ambiguous allusion in *Mental Illness and Psychology* to what he calls a death instinct, the one by which Freud wished to explain the war, although "it was war that was dreamed in this shift in Freud's thinking" (*MI*, p. 83; *MM*, p. 99).

Death alone, along with war, introduces the power of the negative into psychology and into its evolutionist optimism. On the basis of this experience of death, on the basis of what is called in the final pages of *The Birth of the Clinic* "originary finitude"[18] (a vocabulary and theme that then take over Foucault's text and that always seemed to me difficult to dissociate from Heidegger, who as you know is practically never evoked, or even named, by Foucault),[19] Freud is reintegrated into the modernity out of which *The History of Madness* is written and from which he had been banished at regular intervals. It is by taking account of death as "the concrete a priori of medical experience" that "the beginning of that fundamental relation that binds modern man to his originary finitude" comes about (*B*, pp. 196, 197; *N*, pp. 198, 199). This modern man is also a "Freudian man": "the experience of individuality in modern culture is bound up with that of death: from Hölderlin's Empedocles to Nietzsche's Zarathustra, and on to *Freudian man* [my emphasis], an obstinate relation to death prescribes to the universal its singular face, and lends to each individual the power of being heard forever" (*B*, p. 197; *N*, p. 199). Originary finitude is a finitude that no longer arises out of the infinity of a divine presence. It now unfolds "in the void left by the absence of the gods" (*B*, p. 198; *N*, p. 200). What we have here, then, is, in the name of death, so to speak, a reinscription of Freudian man into a "modern" grouping or whole from which he was sometimes excluded.

One can then follow *two* new but equally ambiguous *consequences*. *On the one hand*, the grouping in question will be restructured. One should not be surprised to see reappear, as on the very last page of *The Birth of the Clinic*, the name of Jackson—and, before him, Bichat, whose *Traité des membranes* (1827) and *Recherches physiologiques* would have allowed death to be seen and thought. This vitalism would have arisen against the backdrop of "'mortalism'" (*B*, p. 145; *N*, p. 147). It would be a characteristic of the entire European nineteenth century, and it could be attested to just as well by Goya, Géricault, Delacroix, or Baudelaire, to name a few: "The importance of Bichat, Jackson, and Freud in European culture does not prove that they were philosophers as well as doctors, but that, in this culture, medical thought is fully engaged in the philosophical status of man" (*B*, p. 198; *N*, p. 200).

But there is a second ambiguous consequence of this relation to death as originary finitude. And so, *on the other hand*, the figure or face that is then fixed, and in which one believes one recognizes the traits of "Freudian man," comes to occupy a rather singular place with respect to what Foucault calls the analytic of finitude and the modern *episteme* at the end of *Les Mots et les choses* (*The Order of Things*) (1966). From the standpoint of a certain epistemological trihedron (life, work, and language, or biology, economy, and philology), the human sciences are seen to be at once *inclusive* and *exclusive*; these are Foucault's words (see *OT*, p. 347; *MC*, p. 358).

As for this inclusive exclusion, Freud's work, to which Foucault unwaveringly assigns a model that is more philological than biological, still occupies the place of the *hinge*. Foucault in fact speaks about the place and workings of a "*pivot*": "all this knowledge, within which Western culture had given itself in one century a certain image of man, *pivots* [my emphasis] on the work of Freud, though without, for all that, leaving its fundamental arrangement" (*OT*, p. 361; *MC*, p. 372).

"Though without, for all that, leaving its fundamental arrangement": that is how everything turns round the event or the invention of psychoanalysis. It turns in circles and in place, endlessly returning to the same. It is a revolution that changes nothing. Hence this is not, as Foucault adds at this point, "the most decisive importance of psychoanalysis."

In what, then, does this "most decisive importance of psychoanalysis" consist? In exceeding both consciousness and representation—and, as a result, the human sciences, which do not go beyond the realm of the representable. It is in this respect that psychoanalysis, like ethnology, in fact, does not belong to the field of the human sciences. It "relates the knowledge of man to the finitude that gives man its foundation" (*OT*, p. 381; *MC*, p. 392). We are far from its earlier determination as an analytic psychology. This excessive character leads psychoanalysis toward the forms of finitude that Foucault writes in capital letters, that is, toward Death, Desire, Law or Law-Language (see *OT*, p. 375; *MC*, p. 386). It would be necessary to devote a more detailed and more probing reading to these few pages, something I cannot do here. To keep to the surest schema, let us simply say that, from this point of view and at least to this degree, psychoanalysis, as an analytic of finitude, is now granted an intimacy with the madness that it had sometimes been conceded but had most often been emphatically denied in *The History of Madness*. And this intimacy is a sort of complicity with the madness of the day, the madness of today, "madness in its present form, madness as it is posited in the modern experience, as its truth and its alterity" (*OT*, p. 375; *MC*, p. 387).

But let us not oversimplify things. What Foucault generously grants psychoanalytic experience is now nothing other than what is denied it; more precisely, it sees itself given over to what is denied to it. Indeed, the only privilege that is here granted to psycho-analysis is that of the experience that accedes to that to which it can never accede. If Foucault here mentions, under the name of madness, only schizophrenia and psychosis, it is because psychoanalysis most often approaches these only in order to acknowledge its own limit: a forbidden or impossible access. This limit defines psychoanalysis. Its intimacy with madness par excellence is an intimacy with the least intimate, a nonintimacy that relates it to what is most heterogenous, to that which in no way lets itself be interiorized, nor even subjectified: neither alienated, I would say, nor inalienable.

This is why psychoanalysis finds in that madness *par excellence* ["madness *par excellence*" is also the title given by Blanchot many years earlier to a text on Hölderlin, and Foucault is no doubt echoing this without saying so]—which psychiatrists term schizophrenia—its intimate, its most invincible torture: for, given in this form of madness, in an absolutely manifest and absolutely withdrawn form [this absolute identity of the manifest and the withdrawn, of the open and the secret, is no doubt the key to this double gesture of interpretation and evaluation], are the forms of finitude towards which it usually advances unceasingly (and interminably) from the starting-point of that which is voluntarily-involuntarily offered to it in the patient's language. So psychoanalysis "recognizes itself" when it is confronted with those very psychoses to which, nevertheless (or rather, for that very reason), it has scarcely any means of access: as if the psychosis were displaying in a savage illumination, and offering in a mode not too distant but precisely too close, that towards which analysis must make its laborious way. (*OT*, pp. 375–76; *MC*, p. 387)

This displacement, as ambiguous as it is, leads Foucault to adopt the exact opposite position of certain theses of *The History of Madness* and *Mental Illness and Psychology* concerning the couple patient-doctor, concerning transference or alienation. This time, psychoanalysis not only has nothing to do with a psychology, but it constitutes neither a general theory of man—since it is above all else a knowledge linked to a practice—nor an anthropology (see *OT*, pp. 376, 378–79; *MC*, pp. 388, 390). Even better: in the

movement where he clearly affirms this, Foucault challenges the
very thing of which he had unequivocally accused psychoanalysis,
namely, of being a mythology and a thaumaturgy. He now wants to
explain why psychologists and philosophers were so quick, and so
naive, to denounce a Freudian mythology there where that which
exceeds representation and consciouness must have in fact *resembled*, but only resembled, something mythological (see *OT*, p. 374;
MC, p. 386). As for the thaumaturgy of transference, the logic of
alienation, and the subtly or sublimely asylumlike violence of the
analytic situation, they are no longer, Foucault now says, essential
to psychoanalysis, no longer "constitutive" of it. It is not that all
violence is absent from this rehabilitated psychoanalysis, but it is, I
hardly dare say it, a good violence, or in any case what Foucault
calls a "calm" violence, one that, in the singular experience of
singularity, allows access to "the concrete figures of finitude":

> neither hypnosis, nor the patient's alienation within the fantasmatic
> character of the doctor, is constitutive of psychoanalysis; . . . the latter
> can be deployed only in the calm violence of a particular relationship
> [*rapport singulier*] and the transference it produces. . . . Psychoanalysis
> makes use of the particular relation [*rapport singulier*] of the trans-
> ference in order to reveal, on the outer confines of representation,
> Desire, Law, and Death, which outline, at the extremity of analytic
> language and practice, the concrete figures of finitude. (*OT*, pp. 377–
> 78; *MC*, pp. 388–89)

Things have indeed changed—or so it appears—between *The
History of Madness* and *The Order of Things*.

Whence comes the theme of finitude that seems to govern this
new displacement of the pendulum? To what philosophical event is
this analytic of finitude to be attributed—this analytic in which is
inscribed the trihedron of knowledges or models of the modern
episteme, with its nonsciences, the "'human sciences,'" according
to Foucault (*OT*, p. 366; *MC*, p. 378), and its "'counter-sciences,'"
which Foucault says psychoanalysis and ethnology also are (*OT*,
p. 379; *MC*, p. 391)?

As a project, the analytic of finitude would belong to the tradition of the Kantian critique. Foucault insists on this Kantian filiation by specifying, to cite it once again: "We think in that place." Here is again and for a time, according to Foucault, *our* age, *our* contemporaneity. It is true that if originary finitude obviously makes us think of Kant, it would be unable to do so alone, that is—to summarize an enormous venture in a word, in a name—without the active interpretation of the Heideggerian repetition and all its repercussions, particularly, since this is our topic today, in the discourse of French philosophy and psychoanalysis, and especially, Lacanian psychoanalysis; and when I say Lacanian, I am also referring to all the debates *with* Lacan during the past few decades. This would have perhaps deserved some mention here on the part of Foucault, especially when he speaks of originary finitude. For Kantian finitude is precisely not "originary," as is, on the contrary, the one to which the Heideggerian interpretation leads. Finitude in Kant's sense is instead derived, as is the intuition bearing the same name. But let us leave all this aside, since it would, as we say, take us a bit too far afield.

The "we" who is saying "we think in that place" is evidently, tautologically, the "we" out of which the signatory of these lines, the author of *The History of Madness* and *The Order of Things*, speaks, writes, and thinks. But this "we" never stops dividing, and the places of its signature are displaced in being divided up. A certain untimeliness always disturbs the contemporary who reassures him or herself in a "we." This "we," our "we," is not its own contemporary. The self-identity of its age, or of any age, appears as divided, and thus problematic, *problematizable* (I underscore this word for a reason that will perhaps become apparent in a moment), as the age of madness or an age of psychoanalysis—as well as, in fact, all the historical or archaeological categories that promise us the determinable stability of a configurable whole. Moreover, from the moment a couple separates, from the moment, for example, just to locate here a symptom or a simple indication, the couple Freud/Nietzsche forms and then unforms, this decoupling fissures the identity of the epoch, of the age, of the *episteme* or the paradigm of which one or the other, or both together, might have been the signifiers or representatives. This is even more true when this decoupling comes to fissure the self-identity of some individual, or some presumed individuality, for example, of Freud. What allows one to presume the non–self-difference of Freud, for example? And of psychoanalysis? These decouplings and self-differences no doubt introduce a good deal of disorder into the unity of any configuration, whole, epoch, or historical age. Such disturbances make the historians' work rather uncomfortable, even and especially the work of the most original and refined among them. This self-difference, this difference *to self* [*à soi*], and not simply *with self*, makes life hard if not impossible for historical science. But inversely, would there be any history, would anything ever *happen*, without this principle of disturbance? Would there ever be any event without this disturbance of the principality?

At the point where we are, the age of finitude is being de-identified for at least one reason, from which I can here only abstract the general schema: the thought of finitude, as the thought of finite man, speaks *both* of the tradition, the memory of the Kantian critique or of the knowledges rooted in it, *and* of the end [*fin*] of this finite man, this man who is "nearing its end," as Foucault's most famous sentence would have it in this final wager, placed on the edge of a promise that has yet to take shape, in the final lines of *The Order of Things*: "then one can certainly wager that man would be effaced, like a face drawn in sand at the edge or limit of the sea" (*OT*, p. 387; *MC*, p. 398). The *trait* (the trait of the face, the line or the limit) that then runs the risk of being effaced in the sand would perhaps also be the one that separates an end from itself, thereby multiplying it endlessly and making it, once again, into a limit: the self-relation of a limit at once erases and multiplies the limit; it cannot but divide it in inventing it. The limit only comes to be effaced—it only comes to efface itself—as soon as it is inscribed.

2. *Freud's evil "good genius."* I'm finished with this point, and so I should really finish it up right here. Assuming that I haven't already worn out your patience, I will conclude with a second indication as

a sort of *postscript*—and even more schematically—in order to point once again in the direction of psychoanalysis and to put these hypotheses to the test of *The History of Sexuality* (1976–1984).[20] If one is still willing to follow this figure of the pendulum [*balancier*] making a scene in front of psychoanalysis, then one will observe that the *fort/da* here gives a new impetus to the movement, a movement with the same rhythm but with a greater amplitude and range than ever before. Psychoanalysis is here reduced to a very circumscribed and dependent moment in a history of the "strategies of knowledge and power" (juridical, familial, psychiatric) (*HS*, p. 159; *VS*, p. 210). Psychoanalysis is taken by and interested in these strategies, but it does not think them through. The praises of Freud fall decisively and irreversibly: one hears, for example, of "how wonderfully effective he was—worthy of the greatest spiritual fathers and directors of the classical period—in giving a new impetus to the secular injunction to study sex and transform it into discourse" (*HS*, p. 159; *VS*, p. 210). This time, in other words, in reinscribing the invention of psychoanalysis into the history of a disciplinary dynamic, one no longer indicts only the ruses of objectivization and psychiatric alienation, as in *The History of Madness*, and no longer only the stratagems that would have allowed the *confinement without confinement* of the patient in the invisible asylum of the analytic situation. This time, it is a question of going much further back, and more radically than the "repressive hypothesis" ever did, toward the harsh ruses of the monarchy of sex and the effect of power that supports it. This effect invests in and takes charge of sexuality, so that there is no need to oppose, as one so often and naively believes, power and pleasure.

Since we have been following for so long now the obsessive avatars of the Evil Genius, the irresistible, demonic, and metamorphic returns of this quasi-God, of God's second in command, this metempsychotic Satan, we here find Freud himself once again, Freud, to whom Foucault leaves a choice between only two roles: the bad genius and the good one. What we have here is another chiasmus: in the rhetoric of the few lines that I will read in a moment, one is not surprised to see that the accused, the one who is most directly targeted by the indictment—for no matter how much we deny it, we cannot forget that we are dealing here with a trial and a verdict—is the "good genius of Freud" and not his "bad genius." Why so?

In the final pages of the first volume of *The History of Sexuality*, the accusation of pansexualism, which was often leveled against psychoanalysis, naturally comes up. Those most blind in this regard, says Foucault, were not those who denounced pansexualism out of prudishness. Their only error was to have attributed "solely to the *bad genius* [mauvais génie] of Freud what had already gone through a long stage of preparation" (*HS*, p. 159; *VS*, p. 210; my emphasis). The opposite error, the symmetrical lure, corresponds to a more serious mystification. It is the illusion that could be called emancipatory, the aberration of the Enlightenment, the misguided notion on the part of those who believed that Freud, the *"good genius"* of Freud, had finally freed sex from its repression by power. These

> were mistaken concerning the nature of the process; they believed that Freud had at last, through a sudden reversal, restored to sex the rightful share which it had been denied for so long; they had not seen how the *good genius* of Freud had placed it at one of the critical points marked out for it since the eighteenth century by the strategies of knowledge and power, how wonderfully effective he was . . . in giving a new impetus to the secular injunction to study sex and transform it into discourse. (*HS*, p. 159; *VS*, p. 210; my emphasis)[21]

The "good genius" of Freud would thus be worse than the bad one. It would have consisted in getting itself well placed, in spotting the best place in an old strategy of knowledge and power.

5. Problems

Whatever questions it might leave unanswered—and I will speak in just a moment of one it inspires in me—this project appears nonetheless exciting, necessary, and courageous. I would not want any particular reservation on my part to be too quickly classified among the reactions of those who hastened to defend the threat-ened privilege of the pure invention of psychoanalysis, that is, of an invention that would be *pure*, of a psychoanalysis that one might still dream would have innocently sprung forth already outfitted, helmeted, armed, in short, outside all history, after the epistemo-logical cutting of the cord, as one used to say, indeed, after the unraveling of the navel of the dream. Foucault himself, during an interview, seemed to be ready for some sort of compromise on this issue, readily and good-spiritedly acknowledging the "impasses" (this was his word) of his concept of *episteme* and the difficulties into which this new project had led him.[22] But only those who work, only those who take risks in working, encounter difficulties. One only ever thinks and takes responsibility—if indeed one ever does—by undergoing the aporia; without this, one is content to follow an inclination or apply a program. And it would not be very generous, indeed it would be especially naive and imprudent, to take advantage of these avowals, to take them literally, and to forget what Foucault himself tells us about the confessional scene.

The question that I would have liked to formulate would thus aim neither to protect psychoanalysis against some new attack nor to cast the slightest doubt upon the importance, necessity, and legitimacy of Foucault's extremely interesting project concerning this great history of sexuality. My question would only seek—and this would be, in sum, a sort of modest contribution—to compli-cate somewhat an axiomatic and, on the basis of this, perhaps, certain discursive or conceptual procedures, particularly regarding the way in which this axiomatic is inscribed in its age, in the historical field that serves as a point of departure, and in its reference to psychoanalysis. In a word, without compromising in the least the necessity of reinscribing almost "all" psychoanalysis (assuming one could seriously say such a thing, which I do not believe one can: psychoanalysis *itself*, *all* psychoanalysis, *the whole truth about all* psychoanalysis) into a history that precedes and exceeds it, it would be a question of becoming interested in certain gestures, in certain works, in certain moments of certain works of psychoanalysis, Freudian and post-Freudian (for one cannot, especially in France, seriously treat this subject by limiting oneself to a strictly Freudian discourse and apparatus), in certain traits of a consequently nonglobalizable psychoanalysis, one that is divided and multiple (like the powers that Foucault ceaselessly reminds us are essentially dispersed). It would then be a question of admitting that these necessarily fragmentary or disjointed movements say and do, provide resources for saying and doing, what *The History of Sexuality* (*The Will to Knowledge*) wishes to say, what it *means* [veut dire], and what it wishes to do (to know and to make known) with regard to psychoanalysis. In other words, if one still wanted to speak in terms of age—something that I would only ever do in the form of citation—at this point, here on this line, concerning some trait that is on the side out of which the history of sexuality is written rather than on the side of what it describes or objectifies, one would have to say that Foucault's project in its possibility belongs too much to "the age of psychoanalysis" for it, when claiming to thematize psychoanalysis, to do anything other than let psychoanalysis continue to speak obliquely of itself and to mark one of its folds in a scene that I will not call self-referential or specular but whose structural complication I will not here try to describe (I have tried to do this elsewhere). This is not only because of what withdraws this history from the regime of representation (because of what already inscribes the possibility of this history in and after the age of Freud and Heidegger—to use these names as mere indications for the sake of convenience). It is also for a reason that interests us here more directly: what Foucault announces and denounces about the relation between pleasure and power, in what he calls the "double impetus: pleasure and power" (*HS*, p. 45; *VS*, p. 62), would find, already in Freud, to say nothing of those who followed, discussed, transformed, and displaced him, the very resources for the objection leveled against the "good genius," the so very bad "good genius," of the father of psychoanalysis. I will situate this with just a word in order to conclude.

Foucault clearly cautioned us: this history of sexuality was not to be a historian's history. A "genealogy of desiring man" was to be neither a history of representations nor a history of behaviors or sexual practices. This would lead one to think that sexuality cannot become an object of history without seriously affecting the historian's practice and the concept of history. Moreover, Foucault puts quotation marks around the word *sexuality*: "the quotation marks have a certain importance," he adds.[23] We are thus also dealing here with the history of a word, with its usages starting in the nineteenth century and the reformulation of the vocabulary in relation to a large number of other phenomena, from biological mechanisms to traditional and new norms, to the institutions that support these, be they religious, juridical, pedagogical, or medical (for example, psychoanalytic).

This history of the uses of a word is neither nominalist nor essentialist. It concerns procedures and, more precisely, zones of "problematization." It is a "history of truth" as a history of *problematizations*, and even as an "archeology of problematizations," "through which being offers itself as something that can and must be thought."[24] The point is to analyze not simply behaviors, ideas, or ideologies but, above all, the *problematizations* in which a thought of being intersects "practices" and "practices of the self," a "genealogy of practices of the self" through which these problematizations are formed. With its reflexive vigilance and care in thinking itself in its rigorous specificity, such an analysis thus calls for the *problematization of its own problematization*. And this must *itself* also question itself, with the same archaeological and genealogical care, the same care that it itself methodically prescribes.

When confronted with a historical problematization of such scope and thematic richness, one should not be satisfied either with a mere survey, or with asking in just a few minutes an overarching question so as to insure some sort of synoptic mastery. What we can and must try to do in such a situation is to pay tribute to a work that is this great and this uncertain by means of a question that it itself raises, by means of a question that it carries within itself, that it keeps in reserve in its unlimited potential, one of the questions that can thus be deciphered within it, a question that keeps it in suspense, holding its breath [*tient . . . en haleine*]—and, thus, keeps it alive.

For me one of these questions, for example, would be the one I tried to formulate a few years ago during a conference honoring Foucault at New York University.[25] It was developed by means of a problematization of the concept of power and of the theme of what Foucault calls the *spiral* in the duality power/pleasure. Leaving aside the huge question of the concept of power and of what gives it its alleged unity under the essential dispersion rightly recalled by Foucault himself, I will pull out only a thread: it would lead to that which, in a certain Freud and at the center of a certain French heritage of Freud, would not only never let itself be objectified by the Foucauldian problematization but would actually contribute to it in the most determinate and efficient way, thereby deserving to be inscribed on the thematizing rather than on the thematized border of this history of sexuality. I wonder what Foucault would have said, in this perspective and were he to have taken this into account, not of "Freud" or of psychoanalysis "itself" *in general*— which does not exist any more than power does as one big central and homogeneous corpus—but, for example, since this is only one example, about an undertaking like *Beyond the Pleasure Principle*, about something in its lineage or between its filial connections— along with everything that has been inherited, repeated, or discussed from it since then. In following one of these threads or filial connections, one of the most discreet, in following the abyssal, unassignable, and unmasterable strategy of this text, a strategy that is finally without strategy, one begins to see that this text not only opens up the horizon of a beyond of the pleasure principle (the hypothesis of such a beyond never really seeming to be of interest to Foucault) against which the whole economy of pleasure needs to be rethought, complicated, pursued in its most unrecognizable ruses and detours. By means of one of these filiations—another one unwinding the spool of the *fort/da* that continues to interest us— this text also problematizes, in its greatest radicality, the agency of power and mastery. In a discreet and difficult passage, an original drive for power or drive for mastery (*Bemächtigungstrieb*) is mentioned. It is very difficult to know if this drive for power is still dependent upon the pleasure principle, indeed, upon sexuality as such, upon the austere monarchy of sex that Foucault denounces on the last page of his book.

How would Foucault have situated this drive for mastery in his discourse on power or on irreducibly plural powers? How would he have read this drive, had he read it, in this extremely enigmatic text of Freud? How would he have interpreted the recurring references to the demonic from someone who then makes himself, according to his own terms, the "devil's advocate" and who becomes interested in the hypothesis of a late or derived appearance of sex and sexual pleasure? In the whole problematization whose history he describes, how would Foucault have inscribed this passage from *Beyond the Pleasure Principle*, and this concept and these questions (with all the debates to which this book of Freud either directly or indirectly gave rise, in a sort of overdetermining capitalization, particularly in the France of our age, beginning with everything in Lacan that takes its point of departure in the repetition compulsion [*Wiederholungszwang*])? Would he have inscribed this problematic matrix *within* the whole whose history he describes? Or would he have put it on the other side, on the side of what allows one, on the contrary, to delimit the whole, indeed to problematize it? And thus on a side that no longer belongs to the whole, nor, I would be tempted to think, to any whole, such that the very idea of a gathering of problematization or procedure [*dispositif*], to say nothing any longer of age, *episteme*, paradigm, or epoch, would make for so many problematic names, just as problematic as the very idea of problematization?

This is one of the questions that I would have liked to ask him. I am trying, since this is, unfortunately, the only recourse left us in the solitude of questioning, to imagine the principle of the reply. It would perhaps be something like this: what one must stop believing in is principality or principleness, in the problematic of the principle, in the principled unity of pleasure and power, or of some drive that is thought to be more originary than the other. The theme of the *spiral* would be that of a drive duality (power/pleasure) that is *without principle*.

Is not what Freud was looking for, under the names "death

drive" and "repetition compulsion," that which, coming "before" the principle (of pleasure or reality), would remain forever heterogeneous to the principle of principle?

It is *the spirit of this spiral* that keeps one in suspense, holding one's breath—and, thus, keeps one alive.

The question would thus once again be given a new impetus: is not the duality in question, this spiraled duality, what Freud tried to oppose to all monisms by speaking of a dual drive and of a death drive, of a death drive that was no doubt not alien to the drive for mastery? And, thus, to what is most alive in life, to its very living on [*survivance*]?

I am still trying to imagine Foucault's response. I can't quite do it. I would have so much liked for him to take it on himself.

But in this place where no one now can answer for him, in the absolute silence where we remain nonetheless turned toward him, I would venture to wager that, in a sentence that I will not construct for him, he would have associated and yet also dissociated, he would have sent them packing back to back, mastery and death, that is, the same—death *and* the master, death *as* the master.

Notes

1: Resistances

NOTE: A lecture delivered at the Sorbonne on the occasion of a Franco-Peruvian colloquium organized by the Collège International de Philosophie and the Universities of Strasbourg II and Toulouse le Mirail, from October 30 to November 6, 1991, entitled "The Notion of Analysis." It followed a lecture by Miguel Guisti, to which it alludes several times. A first version of this text appeared in the acts of the colloquium: *La notion d'analyse* (Toulouse: Presses Universitaires du Mirail, 1992). Our thanks to Gérard Granel and Elisabeth Rigal, as well as to the Presses Universitaires du Mirail, for authorizing us to reproduce the slightly modifed text of this lecture.

1. [Sigmund Freud, *The Interpretation of Dreams*, trans. James Strachey, in *The Complete Psychological Works of Sigmund Freud*, vol. 4 (London: Hogarth Press, 1953), n. 1, p. 111. Later page references to this volume will be given in the text. Freud's note says: "I had a feeling that the interpretation of this part of the dream was not carried far enough to make it possible to follow the whole of its concealed meaning. If I had pursued my comparison between the three women, it would have taken me far afield.—There is at least one spot in every dream at which it is unplumbable—a navel, as it were, that is its point of contact with the unknown."—Trans.]

2. Jacques Lacan, *The Four Fundamental Concepts of Psycho-Analysis*, ed. Jacques-Alain Miller, trans. Alan Sheridan (New York: W. W. Norton, 1981), p. 23.

3. [In the French: "qui institue qu'on *doit ne pas* aller au-delà ou, si

vous préférez, qu'on *ne doit pas* aller au-delà parce que cela n'a pas de sens."—Trans.]

4. Samuel Weber, *The Legend of Freud* (Minneapolis: University of Minnesota Press, 1982), pp. 65–83.

5. [Sigmund Freud and Joseph Breuer, *Studies on Hysteria*, in *The Standard Edition of the Complete Psychological Works of Sigmund Freud*, vol. 2 (London: Hogarth Press, 1955), p. 269. Later page references will be given in the text.—Trans.]

6. [This emphasis on the definite article in "*la* psychanalyse" cannot be rendered because English would not use any article before a general abstract noun. The sense here is not that there is more than one psychoanalysis, but that there is not psychoanalysis, no unified concept of psychoanalysis.—Trans.]

7. "Pas," in Derrida, *Parages* (Paris: Galilée, 1986), esp. ca. p. 74.

8. The necessity of this genealogy must always be complicated with a "counter-genealogy." Simple genealogy always risks privileging the archeo-genetic motif, or even the at least symbolic schema of filiation, family, or national origin. On this point, and particularly on the figure of the brother and fraternization, see my *Politiques de l'amitié* (Paris: Galilée, 1994).

9. Derrida, "Plato's Pharmacy," trans. Barbara Johnson, in *Dissemination* (Chicago: University of Chicago Press, 1981), pp. 169–70.

10. I have tried to show this in *Limited Inc*, trans. Samuel Weber (Evanston: Northwestern University Press, 1988), esp. pp. 127–28.

11. See my "To Speculate—on 'Freud,'" in *The Post Card: From Socrates to Freud and Beyond*, trans. Alan Bass (Chicago: University of Chicago Press, 1987), p. 396, for example.

12. Ibid., pp. 260 and 387.

13. See *Dissemination*, esp. "Outwork," p. 26.

14. This alternative can take on the guise of sacrifice. Everything, then, would perhaps happen between sacrifice and nonsacrifice, unless it remains suspended—in the *approach*—between the sacrifice that *knots* and the sacrifice that *cuts*, in sum, the two great experiences of Isaac and Abraham. Once again the idiom, the idiom of resistance and the resistance of the idiom: not only of that which belongs properly to the origin, to God, to the Father, or to the Son, but of the right to translate this scene, the name of this scene, in an essentially approaching fashion, by the distant word "sacrifice."

2: *For the Love of Lacan*

NOTE: This is the transcription of a paper read at the colloquium entitled *Lacan avec les philosophes* at UNESCO, sponsored by the Collège International de Philosophie in May 1990. The tone, which was that of quasi-improvisation, has been preserved as far as possible. This text was first published in *Lacan avec les philosophes* the same year by Albin Michel, and we thank them for having authorized this reprinting. Delivered during the last session of the conference, "For the Love of Lacan" was intended first of all as a response to lectures by René Major, "Depuis Lacan," and by Stephen Melville, "Depuis Lacan?" A reading of these two lectures, in the acts of the colloquium, will clarify several allusions and indeed the general orientation of this text. As for the debates that surrounded, preceded, and followed this lecture, I likewise refer the reader to the "Annexes (Correspondance et Post-scriptum)" published in the same volume (pp. 421–52).

1. Jacques Lacan, *The Four Fundamental Concepts of Psychoanalysis*, cited in Major, "Depuis Lacan," p. 387.

2. Major, "Depuis Lacan," p. 387.

3. On this condition, I refer the reader to the "Annexes (Correspondance et Post-Scriptum)" published in *Lacan avec les philosophes*, pp. 422–52.

4. [Jacques Lacan, "Seminar on 'The Purloined Letter,'" trans. Jeffrey Mehlman, in John P. Muller and William J. Richardson, eds., *The Purloined Poe: Lacan, Derrida, and Psychoanalytic Reading* (Baltimore: Johns Hopkins University Press, 1988), p. 28. The "Seminar" is not included in the selection from *Ecrits* edited and translated by Alan Sheridan (New York: W. W. Norton, 1977). According to Sheridan, this selection was approved by Lacan himself.—Trans.]

5. [Derrida is referring to the then recently published novel by Julia Kristeva, *Les Samouraï* (Paris: Grasset, 1989).—Trans.]

6. Elisabeth Roudinesco, *Jacques Lacan and Co.: A History of Psychoanalysis in France, 1925–1985*, trans. Jeffrey Mehlman (Chicago: University of Chicago Press, 1990), pp. 410–11.

7. [Jacques Lacan, "Présentation," in *Ecrits* (Paris: Seuil, 1966), p. 11. This new introduction is dated 1969 and was written for the paperback edition of *Ecrits*.—Trans.]

8. Derrida, "De la grammatologie," *Critique*, 223 and 224 (December

1965, January 1966): 16–42 and 23–53; *De la grammatologie* (Paris: Minuit, 1967).

9. Derrida, *Positions*, trans. Alan Bass (Chicago: University of Chicago Press, 1981), p. 111, n. 44.

10. Lacan, "Seminar on 'The Purloined Letter,'" p. 43; French ed., p. 29; emphasis added.

11. Ibid., p. 50; French ed., p. 38.

12. Lacan, "Propos sur la causalité psychique," in *Ecrits*, p. 193.

13. Lacan, "The Function and Field of Speech and Language in Psychoanalysis," in *Ecrits*, p. 98; French ed., p. 313.

14. [The anterior placement of the adjective *vraie* suggests a more fundamental quality of the trueness of speech than when it is in the posterior position.—Trans.]

15. Lacan, "Variantes de la cure-type," in *Ecrits*, p. 351.

16. Lacan, "Function and Field of Speech," p. 48; French ed., p. 256.

17. Ibid., p. 88; French ed., p. 302.

18. Ibid., p. 49; French ed., p. 258.

19. Lacan, "Réponse au commentaire de Jean Hyppolite sur la 'Verneinung' de Freud," in *Ecrits*, p. 381.

20. Lacan, "The Signification of the Phallus," in *Ecrits*, p. 287; French ed., p. 692.

21. Lacan, "La science et la vérité," in *Ecrits*, p. 877.

22. Lacan, "Situation de la psychanalyse et formation du psychanalyste en 1956," in *Ecrits*, p. 470.

23. Lacan, "Seminar on 'The Purloined Letter,'" p. 53; French ed., p. 41.

24. Ibid., p. 39; French ed., p. 24.

25. Lacan, "A Jakobson," in *Le Séminaire, Livre XX: Encore* (Paris: Seuil, 1975), p. 22.

26. [Derrida, *The Post Card: From Socrates to Freud and Beyond*, trans. Alan Bass (Chicago: University of Chicago Press, 1987), p. 482. Later page references to this book will be given in the text.—Trans.]

27. Lacan, "De Rome 53 à Rome 67: La psychanalyse. Raisons d'un échec," in *Scilicet*, June 17, 1968, p. 47.

28. [The reference is to Derrida's "Fors: Les mots anglés de Nicolas Abraham et Maria Torok," a foreword to Abraham and Torok, *Cryptonomie: Le Verbier de l'Homme aux loups* (Paris: Aubier-Montaigne, 1976); "Fors: The Anglish Words of Nicolas Abraham and Maria Torok," trans. Barbara Johnson, in Abraham and Torok, *The Wolf Man's Magic*

Word: A Cryptonomy (Minneapolis: University of Minnesota Press, 1986).
For an account of the episode, see Roudinesco, *Jacques Lacan and Co.*,
pp. 592–94.—Trans.]

3: *"To Do Justice to Freud"*

N O T E : A lecture delivered in the Main Amphitheater of Sainte-Anne
Hospital on November 23, 1991, on the occasion of the thirtieth anniversary of the publication of Foucault's *Folie et déraison: Histoire de la folie à
l'âge classique*. At the initiative of Elisabeth Roudinesco and René Major,
the meeting was organized as the Ninth Colloquium of the International
Society for the History of Psychiatry and Psychoanalysis. It was opened
by Georges Canguilhem. The first version of this text was initially
published in the acts of the colloquium: *Penser la folie, essais sur Michel
Foucault* (Paris: Galilée, 1992).

1. [See Michel Foucault, *Folie et déraison: Histoire de la folie à l'âge
classique* (Paris: Plon, 1961), pp. 53–57; hereafter abbreviated *F*. Derrida
refers here and throughout to the original edition of this work. When the
book was reprinted with different pagination in 1972, "Mon corps, ce
papier, ce feu," Foucault's response to Derrida's "Cogito et histoire de la
folie," was added as an appendix. This lecture by Derrida was first given
in 1963. It was reprinted in 1967 in Derrida, *L'écriture et la différence*
(Paris: Seuil, 1967). A much abridged version of *Histoire de la folie* was
published in 1964 and was translated into English by Richard Howard
under the title *Madness and Civilization: A History of Insanity in the Age of
Reason* (New York: Random House, 1965); hereafter abbreviated *M*.
Since Derrida refers to the unabridged text of 1961 and works with the
original title throughout, we have referred to this work as *The History of
Madness* (or, in some cases, *The History of Madness in the Classical Age*).
This is in keeping with "Cogito and the History of Madness," *Writing
and Difference*, trans. Alan Bass (Chicago: University of Chicago Press,
1978), pp. 31–63. For the reader who wishes to follow Derrida's itinerary
through *Folie et déraison: Histoire de la folie à l'âge classique*, we have given
references to the 1961 French version along with references to the English
translation when they exist in the abridged version. Since all the other
texts of Foucault cited by Derrida have been translated in their entirety,
we have in each case given the English followed by the French page
references. Translations have been slightly modified in several instances
to fit the context of Derrida's argument.—Trans.]

2. [Derrida, "Cogito and the History of Madness," *Writing and Differ-ence*, p. 38; "Cogito et histoire de la folie," *L'écriture et la différence*, p. 61.
3. See ibid., p. 307; p. 53.—Trans.]
4. [See Jacques Lacan, "Propos sur la causalité psychique" and "La Science et la vérité," *Ecrits* (Paris: Seuil, 1966), p. 209, pp. 219–44. The latter essay was translated by Bruce Fink under the title "Science and Truth," *Newsletter of the Freudian Field* 3, nos. 1–2 (1989): 4–29.—Trans.]
5. Lacan, "Propos sur la causalité psychique," *Ecrits*, p. 193.
6. [This final chapter of *Histoire de la folie* is not included in *Madness and Civilization*.—Trans.]
7. [This is so for the French versions but not for the English.—Trans.]
8. I note in passing that we have here, along with very brief allusions to *Three Essays on the Theory of Sexuality, Introductory Lectures on Psycho-Analysis*, a couple of individual cases in *Mental Illness and Psychology*, and an equally brief reference to *Totem and Taboo* in *The Order of Things*, one of the few times that Foucault mentions a work by Freud; beyond this, he does not, to my knowledge, cite or analyze any text by Freud, or by any other psychoanalyst, not even those of contemporary French psycho-analysts. Each time, only the proper name "Freud" or the common name "psychoanalysis" is pronounced. See Michel Foucault, *Maladie mentale et psychologie* (Paris: Presses Universitaires de France, 1962), hereafter ab-breviated *MM*, trans. Alan Sheridan as *Mental Illness and Psychology* (Berkeley: University of California Press, 1987), p. 31, hereafter abbrevi-ated *MI*; and *Les Mots et les choses: Une archéologie des sciences humaines* (Paris: Gallimard, 1966), hereafter abbreviated *MC*, trans. as *The Order of Things: An Archaeology of the Human Sciences* (New York: Random House, 1973), p. 379, hereafter abbreviated *OT*.
Discovery is underscored by Foucault, along with *return* and *language*. Freud is the event of a *discovery*—the unconscious and psychoanalysis as a movement of *return*—and what relates the discovery to the return is language, the possibility of speaking with madness, "the possibility of a dialogue with unreason."
9. Foucault earlier noted this in *F*, p. 195.
10. Foucault, "My Body, This Paper, This Fire," trans. Geoff Ben-nington, *Oxford Literary Review* 4 (Autumn 1979): 26; trans. "Mon corps, ce papier, ce feu" was first published in *Paideia* (September 1971); it was reissued as the appendix to the 1972 edition of *Histoire de la folie*.
11. Derrida, "Cogito and the History of Madness," *Writing and Differ-ence*, p. 58; "Cogito et histoire de la folie," *L'écriture et la différence*, p. 91.

12. Foucault, "My Body, This Paper, This Fire," p. 26.

13. Foucault, *Raymond Roussel* (Paris: Gallimard, 1963), p. 10; trans. Charles Ruas as *Death and the Labyrinth: The World of Raymond Roussel* (New York: Doubleday, 1986), p. 3.

14. "And so laws keep up their good standing, not because they are just, but because they are laws: that is the mystical foundation of their authority, they have no other. . . . Anyone who obeys them because they are just is not obeying them the way he ought to" (quoted in Derrida, "Force of Law: The 'Mystical Foundation of Authority,'" trans. Mary Quaintance, *Cardozo Law Review* 11 [July-August 1990]: 939; Derrida's French text appears *en face*). Elsewhere, Montaigne mentioned the "legitimate fictions" on which "our law" "founds the truth of its justice" (ibid.). Pascal cites Montaigne without naming him when he recalls both the principle of justice and the fact that it should not be traced back to its source unless one wants to ruin it. What is he himself doing, then, when he speaks of "the mystical foundation of its authority," adding in the same breath, "whoever traces it to its source annihilates it" (ibid.)? Is he re-founding or ruining that of which he speaks? Will one ever know? Must one know?

Power, authority, knowledge and nonknowledge, law, judgment, fiction, good standing or credit, transfer: from Montaigne to Pascal onto others, we recognize the same network of a critical problematic, an active, vigilant, hypercritical problematization. It is difficult to be sure that the "classical age" did not thematize, reflect, and also deploy the concepts of its symptoms: the concepts that one would later direct toward the symptoms that it would one day be believed can be assigned to it.

15. Insofar as, and to the extent that, it follows Jackson's model (for the "stroke of genius" also consists in escaping from this model), psycho-analysis is *credulous*, it *will have been* credulous, for it is in this that it is outdated, a credulous presumption: "it believed that it could," "Freud believed." After having cited Jackson's *The Factors of Insanities*, Foucault adds (I emphasize the verb and tense of *to believe*):

> Jackson's entire work tended to give right of place to evolutionism in neuro- and psycho-pathology. Since the *Croonian Lectures* (1874), it has no longer been possible to omit the regressive aspects of illness; evolution is now one of the dimensions by which one gains access to the pathological fact.
> A whole side of Freud's work consists of a commentary on the evolutionary forms of neurosis. The history of the libido, of its development, of its succes- sive fixations, resembles a collection of the pathological possibilities of the

individual: each type of neurosis is a return to a libidinal stage of evolution. And psychoanalysis *believed that it could* write a psychology of the child by carrying out a pathology of the adult. . . . This is the celebrated Oedipus complex, in which Freud *believed* that he could read the enigma of man and the key to his destiny, in which one must find the most comprehensive analysis of the conflicts experienced by the child in his relations with his parents and the point at which many neuroses became fixated.

In short, every libidinal stage is a potential pathological structure. Neurosis is a spontaneous archeology of the libido. (*MI*, pp. 19–21; *MM*, pp. 23–26)

16. For example: "It is not a question of invalidating the analyses of pathological regression; all that is required is to free them of the myths that neither Janet nor Freud succeeded in separating from them" (*MI*, p. 26; *MM*, p. 31).

17. An identical schema is at work a few pages earlier: "Psychology can never tell the truth about madness because it is madness that holds the truth of psychology." It is again a tragic vision, a tragic discourse on the tragic. Hölderlin, Nerval, Roussel, and Artaud are again named through their works as witnesses of a "tragic confrontation with madness" free of all psychology (*MI*, pp. 74, 75; *MM*, p. 89). No reconciliation is possible between psychology, even if analytic, and tragedy.

18. Foucault, *Naissance de la clinique: Une archéologie du regard médical* (Paris: Presses Universitaires de France, 1963), p. 199; hereafter abbreviated *N*; trans. A. M. Sheridan Smith as *The Birth of the Clinic: An Archeology of Medical Perception* (New York: Random House, 1975), p. 197; hereafter abbreviated *B*.

19. Except perhaps in passing in *Les Mots et les choses*: "the experience of Hölderlin, Nietzsche, and Heidegger, in which the return is posited only in the extreme recession of the origin" (*OT*, p. 334; *MC*, p. 345).

This leaden silence would last, I believe, until an interview given not long before his death. Faithful to the Foucauldian style of interpretation, one might say that the spacing of this omission, of this blank silence—like the silence that reigns over the name of Lacan, whom one can associate with Heidegger up to a certain point, and thus with a few others who never ceased, in France and elsewhere, dialogue with these two—is anything but the empty and inoperative sign of an absence. On the contrary, it *gives rise* or *gives the place* [donne lieu]; it marks out the place and the age. The dotted lines of a suspended writing *situate* with a formidable precision. No attention to the age or to the problem of the age should lose sight of this.

20. [*Histoire de la sexualité* is the name given by Foucault to his entire project on sexuality, of which three volumes have now been published: *La volonté de savoir* (Paris: Gallimard, 1976), hereafter abbreviated *VS*, trans. Robert Hurley as *The History of Sexuality: Volume I, An Introduction* (New York: Random House, 1978), hereafter abbreviated *HS*; *L'usage des plaisirs* (Paris: Gallimard, 1984), trans. Hurley as *The Use of Pleasure: Volume 2 of 'The History of Sexuality'* (New York: Random House, 1985); and *Le souci de soi* (Paris: Gallimard, 1984), trans. Hurley as *The Care of the Self: Volume 3 of 'The History of Sexuality'* (New York: Random House, 1986).—Trans.]

21. It is perhaps appropriate to recall the lines immediately following this, the last in the first volume of *The History of Sexuality*. They unequivocally describe this sort of Christian teleology, or, more precisely, modern Christianity (as opposed to "an old Christianity"), whose completion would, in some sense, be marked by psychoanalysis:

> the secular injunction to study sex and transform it into discourse. We are often reminded of the countless procedures which an old Christianity once employed to make us detest the body; but let us ponder all the ruses that were employed for centuries to make us love sex, to make the knowledge of it desirable and everything said about it precious. Let us consider the stratagems by which we were induced to apply all our skills to discovering its secrets, by which we were attached to the obligation to draw out its truth, and made guilty for having failed to recognize it for so long. These devices are what ought to make us wonder today. Moreover, we need to consider the possibility that one day, perhaps, in a different economy of bodies and pleasures, people will no longer quite understand how the ruses of sexuality, and the power that sustains its organization, were able to subject us to that austere monarchy of sex, so that we became dedicated to the endless task of forcing its secret, of exacting the truest of confessions from a shadow.
>
> The irony of this deployment is in having us believe that our "liberation" is in the balance. (*HS*, p. 159; *VS*, pp. 210–11)

Some might be tempted to relate this conclusion to that of *The Order of Things*, to everything that is said there about the *end* and about its *tomorrow*, about man "nearing his end" right up to this "day" when, as *The History of Sexuality* says, "in a different economy of bodies and pleasures, people will no longer quite understand how," and so on. It is difficult not to hear at least in the rhetoric and tonality of such a call, in the apocalyptic and eschatological tone of this promise (even if "we can at the moment do no more than sense the possibility [of this event]—

without knowing either what its form will be or what it promises" [*OT*, p. 387; *MC*, p. 398]), a certain resonance with the Christianity and Christian humanism whose end is being announced.

22. See "Le Jeu de Michel Foucault," *Ornicar?* 10 (July 1977): 62–93; trans., in a version edited by Alain Grosrichard as "The Confession of the Flesh," *Power/Knowledge: Selected Interviews and Other Writings, 1972–77*, trans. Colin Gordon et al., ed. Colin Gordon (New York: Pantheon, 1980), esp. pp. 196–97.

23. Foucault, *The Use of Pleasure*, p. 3; *L'usage des plaisirs*, p. 9.

24. Ibid., pp. 11–13; pp. 17–19.

25. The following analysis intersects a much longer treatment of the subject in an unpublished paper entitled "Beyond the Power Principle," which I presented at a conference honoring Foucault, organized at New York University by Thomas Bishop in April 1986.

MERIDIAN

Crossing Aesthetics

Massimo Cacciari, *Posthumous People: Vienna at the Turning Point*

David E. Wellbery, *The Specular Moment: Goethe's Early Lyric and the Beginnings of Romanticism*

Edmond Jabès, *The Little Book of Unsuspected Subversion*

Hans-Jost Frey, *Studies in Poetic Discourse: Mallarmé, Baudelaire, Rimbaud, Hölderlin*

Pierre Bourdieu, *The Rules of Art: Genesis and Structure of the Literary Field*

Nicolas Abraham, *Rhythms: On the Work, Translation, and Psychoanalysis*

Jacques Derrida, *On the Name*

David Wills, *Prosthesis*

Maurice Blanchot, *The Work of Fire*

Jacques Derrida, *Points . . . : Interviews, 1974–1994*

J. Hillis Miller, *Topographies*

Philippe Lacoue-Labarthe, *Musica Ficta (Figures of Wagner)*

Jacques Derrida, *Aporias*

Emmanuel Levinas, *Outside the Subject*

Jean-François Lyotard, *Lessons on the Analytic of the Sublime*

Peter Fenves, *"Chatter": Language and History in Kierkegaard*

Jean-Luc Nancy, *The Experience of Freedom*

Jean-Joseph Goux, *Oedipus, Philosopher*

Haun Saussy, *The Problem of a Chinese Aesthetic*

Jean-Luc Nancy, *The Birth to Presence*

Library of Congress Cataloging-in-Publication Data

Derrida, Jacques.
  [Résistances de la psychanalyse. English]
  Resistances of psychoanalysis / Jacques Derrida.
      p.   cm. — (Meridian : crossing aesthetics)
    ISBN 0-8047-3018-0 (cloth : alk. paper)
    ISBN 0-8047-3019-9 (pbk. : alk. paper).
    1. Psychoanalysis.   2. Freud, Sigmund.   3. Lacan,
  Jacques.   4. Foucault, Michel.   5. Resistance (Psychoanalysis)
  I. Title.   II. Series: Meridian (Stanford, Calif.)
  RC509.D47   1998
  150.19'5—dc21   97-45151
                                                          CIP

⊚ This book is printed on acid-free paper.

Original printing 1998
Last figure below indicates year of this printing:
07 06 05 04 03 02 01 00 99 98